Loving and Learning

Life with Lisa and Down Syndrome

Angee Barcus

Loving and Learning

Copyright © 2017 by Angela Barcus All rights reserved.

No part of this book may be reproduced or used in any form without written permission from the author. The only exception is by a reviewer, who may quote short excerpts in a review.

Printed in the United States of America
ISBN-13: 9780997383218

Dedication

First, to Lisa: I am blessed and grateful to have Lisa in my life, because she brings so much joy, has opened up a new world that I would have not experienced without her and truthfully, without her there would be no story.

Second, to my three other children, Tammy, Brent and Adam: They have been one of the main reasons for writing Lisa's story. I want them to remember how we came to be the family we are today.

And finally, to my husband Monte: He is always willing to go golf when I need some quiet time in the house to write. You are my cheerleader, always encouraging me along the way to publication. My deepest love to each and every one of you.

Acknowledgements

Many thanks to those who agreed to proofread this book. I appreciate the time you spent, the positive and helpful comments and the honest feedback you gave.

I also want to say thank you my children and husband, who contributed to this book and who encouraged me along the way. You are all special to me and I am grateful for all you have done to help prepare this book for publication.

Table of Contents

vii   Preface

P.1   Set the Stage
P.17   Bringing Baby Home

P.23   Acceptance
P.29   Welcome to Holland

P.35   Dad's Hair-dos for Lisa
P.39   Hospital Stay

P.45   Discipline: A Challenge
P.53   Summer Plans

P.57   Loosening the Apron Strings
P.61   Lisa as the Teacher

P.65   The Innocent
P.67   People-first Language Encouraged

P.73   Preparing for Regular Education Classes
P.77   Circle of Friends

P.85   Inclusion, Integration, Transition
P.97   A Vacation for the Family

P.103 School Notes, Reports and Quarterly Remarks
P.109 My Baby Sister-A Personal Essay
P.113 Thoughts on Inclusion

P.119 A Mother's Love
P.121 Heaven's Very Special Child
P.123 Our Ups and Downs

P.127 Van Rides
P.137 High School

P.143   Work, Play and School Activities
P.149   Sponsored Child

P.155   More High School
P.159   Manifestation Determination

P.179   Guardianship
P.189   One More High School

P.199   A Great Transition
P.207   Youth Leadership Forum

P.215   Employment Agency
P.219   Health Issues become Work Issues

P.227   Santa Notes from Lisa
P.229   A Rap by Lisa and Other Notes

P.231   "The Life of Me"
P.233   More Notes from Lisa

P.237   Epilogue

Preface

Loving And Learning: Life With Lisa And Down Syndrome is the second book of three. Some of the stories were difficult for me to write and as I wrote them, my feelings of sadness, despair and heartaches rose to the surface. I hope that by reading about these difficult accounts, it will bring some insight to others who might be or have been in the same situations we experienced with Lisa.

Loving and Learning covers topics on Inclusion, Guardianship and the Manifestation Determination process, plus other pertinent issues that deal with Lisa growing up and getting ready for her independence in the real world. As an added bonus, several of Lisa's siblings have included their talents and thoughts as well. One brother writes about how he saw Lisa when she was born and how they connected on their walks together. The other brother was happy to contribute some of his grade school age artwork of Lisa, illustrated through his loving and affectionate approach, of what he saw in Lisa.

Lisa's Dad has agreed to include an article he wrote when asking senators to be aware and mindful of the needs of others, especially when the relevant topic matter was connected to funding programs for people with developmental or intellectual disabilities. Lisa has also contributed to the book, allowing some of her notes, journal thoughts and speeches to be added to the mix of stories. There are also several poems that are very near and dear to my heart, written by authors who have given their permission for their poetry to be included. I feel it is an added bonus to include these special compilations.

Enjoy the book, and thanks for reading!

Set The Stage-A Recap And More

Let's start at the beginning. I want to set the stage for this book and will write a few things that might sound like you've heard them before. In my first book, "Snapshots of Lisa," I briefly revisited Lisa's birth, but before I can tell the rest of the stories about Lisa, I have to relate a few more newborn narrations.

Lisa was born with Down syndrome, a form of mental retardation. Her specific form is called Trisomy 21. At that time, the incidence of babies born with Down syndrome occurred about 1 in 600 to 1 in 700 live births. After she was born, a doctor came in to look at Lisa, checked her weight, color and reaction times. I found out later that she failed the Apgar test. That is a test that checks color, breathing and reactions at birth and at five minutes after birth.

My obstetrician tried to inform me of his suspicions concerning Lisa by pointing to certain characteristics that supported his findings. She had the simian [1] line (or palmar crease) across one palm of her hand. She had the small, flat bridge of a nose, eyes that turned up and funny folds in the eyelids. Also, on her hands, her pinky fingers curved inward more than usual. The doctor also reported x-rays of her hips would be taken and a chromosome blood test done to confirm the diagnosis of Down syndrome.

Later on that day, as the nurses were busy caring for her needs in the nursery, Lisa became dusky and blue in color. It wasn't until a week later, when a cardiologist saw Lisa that it was suspected there was a hole in the bottom section of her heart. The medical diagnosis is a VSD or ventricular septal defect.

The doctor asked me questions about my three other pregnancies, how much they weighed and so on. Lisa's birth weight was 8 pounds 13 ounces, which was considered a large birth weight for a baby with Down syndrome. The doctor's attention was focused on her and I immediately felt something was wrong. When he said Down syndrome, neither my husband nor I knew what this was; but it was made very clear when he said retarded or mongoloid. He did emphasize that those terms were not used much anymore, and I can see why those terms are now considered obsolete. For me, I felt like I was thrown into a wall at sixty miles an hour when I heard our child was retarded or mongoloid. You must remember this was back in the early '80s and the television show "Life Goes On" would not be aired until 1989. Chris Burke, who has Down syndrome, played Corky and the show depicted the challenges that might arise when a family has a child with Down syndrome. The term Down syndrome is much kinder on a parent's ears, mind and heart. I could deny the failed tests at birth, saying she just wasn't as active as most children. I did not see the differences in her nose and eyes, thinking my other children looked like that at birth. I could not wish away the results of x-rays or the blood tests, but until the results were complete and verified for certain, I would continue to deny the impending truth.

Through all the commotion during Lisa's birth and

explanation of the findings that she might have Down syndrome, my mind reeled back to some four months before, when I sat at my other children's grade school, watching an assembly program. I was five months pregnant with Lisa, with an aching back and swollen feet as my only discomforts. I placed my feet on the back of a folding chair in front of me and I watched a group of pre-school children being escorted into the gymnasium. They were taken to the first row for a better view of the stage. This pre-school group was unique for it was an integrated program for children with disabilities to go to a neighborhood school with everyday, typical children. The children that were being brought in to the assembly all had a disability. All needed help in some way. All were unique.

As I watched them enter, I noticed some children had their own specially designed wheelchairs, some children used walkers that dragged noisily across the tiled floor and some children were being carried. They drooled, cried or laughed uncontrollably. They either didn't talk or talked nonsense words. They needed constant attention, constant love and constant nurturing. I silently thanked God for giving me three wonderful, healthy children, knowing positively, without a doubt, that I could never handle a child with a disability. I also feared for the parents and any child who had a disability, not knowing what lie ahead in their future. I whispered my prayer of thanks, unaware that the child I was carrying would be born with Down syndrome. I watched those children a while longer, sad to see their disabilities but confident in the fact that it couldn't possible happen to me. (As a side note: about five years later I would be working as a nurse in that same school building and some of my daily duties included doing occupational and physical therapies for the children in that same classroom. We sure don't know what life has in store for us, do we?) I turned my attention to the stage and quickly forgot about those children. It wasn't until four months later, when I was in the delivery room, a cold, cruel place where I then faced the uncertain future of my daughter. I wanted this to be different, but I could not change what was to be.

Doctors were everywhere at the time of Lisa's birth; in the delivery room, in the hallway and in my private hospital room. My husband was ever at my side, in his own daze of this mess, but was very positive about the situation. The only words from him that I can still hear today were not those of sadness or despair, but a simple statement he repeated over and over. He continually said "That's too bad, that's too bad." I don't know what he meant by those words, but it must have helped him to cope with the spiraling, roller coaster ride we were on. He even maintained his positive attitude when he had the task of telling out-of-town family members about Lisa. How do you tell the grandparents about this wonderful little girl and then add, "But, there's a problem." How do you celebrate with candy or flowers when you don't feel very cheerful? How do you keep up a good front for your wife, when you also feel like crying and asking "Why?" I don't know how, but my husband was able to get through it better than I did.

I remember how hard it was for my husband to call other family members, grandparents and friends, and tell them the good news, (a new baby) the fair news, (she might have Down Syndrome) and the bad news, (a heart problem). Most of those who were called or who came to visit were supportive and caring. I can only think of one or two friends who, when they came to see us and found out about Lisa's disability, left quickly. Maybe they didn't know what to say or ask, but their actions spoke volumes.

One set of grandparents had trouble accepting the long-term outcome. Their comments of "Look how well she's doing" and "She must be getting better" were well meaning, but these words made me sad just the same, for I knew that was not the case. Having Down syndrome was not something that you could recover from. One couple said later on that they suspected something was wrong with Lisa, but had not been told and they were afraid to say anything to us. We have since encouraged them to ask questions, reassuring them that we wanted to share.

My husband held up wonderfully. He was supportive and understanding. I was the one who cried when I thought of Lisa's future. I cried when I saw her. I worried about what to do with her, how to care for and if I could love her. I discovered that loving her was easy. That first time I held her in my arms, I knew I loved her and it made everything better. I was like any other mother, taking off the blanket, counting her toes and fingers, looking at her miniature features and marveling at the perfectly formed child. How could she have Down syndrome? To me, she did not look like she had Down syndrome. I thought, 'The doctors must be wrong.' Denial was there but until they had positive test results, I clung to what little chance there was that she did not have this congenital disability. As I now look back on that episode, the shock and sadness no longer seemed as harsh as I remembered. I can now see it was natural for us to grieve, for we lost the kind of a daughter we had expected would be perfect. Little did we know that there is no such thing as perfect.

As we struggled with our first emotions, doctors threw us into a tailspin with the news of a heart disorder. I silently screamed, "This is so unfair. How could she have any other problems; I mean, she has Down syndrome; isn't that enough for us to handle?" It was definitely obvious she had heart problems when she became dusky and blue in color. I worried she would die in my arms. I cried for her, her health and her uncertain future. My heart ached with sadness. I felt I could not deal with any more problems. I felt that we were alone in this state of affairs we were going through.

It was natural for us to go through the various stages of grief, complete with my mood swings and wild emotions. I can now say I was silly to cry at the sight of Lisa or to wonder how we would care for her but at that time my thoughts were normal for me and for the situation. Would life with Lisa be difficult, embarrassing and fateful or would life be just different, exciting and funny? Would it be sad and changeless or satisfying and ever changing? Unbeknownst to us, Lisa would change us by being a part of our family. I could not and I would not change her for the world. I want to let other parents know there will not always be sad times when you have a child with a disability. Life with Lisa has always been about loving and learning.

We brought Lisa home from the hospital and sat down with the three other children to talk about Lisa. We first talked of the plans we had made to take Lisa into a cardiologist within two days. We told them about Lisa, her disability and heart condition. We let them know they would be cared for while we were gone. We were truthful, but limited the information, knowing they might be too small to understand all of it. Simply spoken by one child was the statement that "retarded just means slow", so she won't learn as fast. What a refreshing, wholesome outlook. And we had tried to carry that thought with us throughout the years. I believe we tried to make each child feel important, especially after we realized our whole lives had suddenly started to revolve around Lisa, so we tried to include special time for each child. They were very accepting of Lisa and proud to have her for a sister. They talked about her to classmates, teachers and others, with all the correct information regarding Down syndrome. They and we were willing to take Lisa anywhere, anytime.

If there was sibling rivalry, it was healthy, normal and of little concern in the grand scheme of things. This was part of their growing up, with or without a sister who has a disability. I feel, at this point in time, they have all adjusted well and definitely do love her for who she is. They were never concerned with her disability and they continue to look at her with acceptance and love as they always have. They are very caring siblings who treat Lisa with dignity, respect and love.

When Lisa was three months old, she was enrolled in a homebound program. School personnel also came to our home for different tests, evaluations and visits before enrolling her into a newborn program. A homebound teacher came two times a week, until she was three years old. We were given daily and weekly activities to work on, such as visual tracking, tactile stimuli and verbal encouragements. She was also visited by a physical therapist, bi-monthly, to help with motor activities. As a family, we also did designated activities with Lisa throughout the week, to help her learn. A speech therapist visited and gave us activities and ideas to use as we could. I remember echoing many repetitions of a sound Lisa would make, and lots of claps and praises when she mastered it. We also did tongue exercises by placing peanut butter on the outer lips or on the roof of her mouth, to encourage more tongue movement. It must have helped Lisa, because her speech is clearly understandable most of the time; a big plus for a person with Down syndrome.

We encouraged the entire family to know what activities we were working on, charted success and failures daily and made almost every situation a learning adventure. She had always been in school, even in the summer. Her only down time was when the school had a two-week break before and after the regular school year, and in between those two well-deserved breaks, Lisa had six to eight weeks of summer school.

Lisa entered a center-based program at the age of three. In this school district, a center-based setting usually meant it was a special ed program housed in a public school building. She attended a school-based program one to two times a week and continued to receive some homebound help. Between the age of three to four, Lisa began a pre-school handicapped program housed at a regular elementary school. At this time, she began to ride the school van. I still remember that first day. I lifted Lisa up to the front seat, buckled her in and gave her the book bag she was using, shut the door and waved good-bye to her. Then, I cried. She was already beginning to grow up; that first step towards her leaving home. That was a difficult and sad realization for me.

In the pre-school setting, they tried some peer modeling by bringing in typical children close to the same ages and who did not have any disabilities. At that time, my youngest son attended as a peer model and he thought that was really neat. At age five, Lisa attended a special educational kindergarten that was also housed in a regular elementary school.

Lisa attended one year of kindergarten, had a mandatory three year evaluation done and was then in an all day, first grade classroom in special education, with part of her day being spent in a regular classroom. She was in a DLP or developmental learning program. She was encouraged to work on the academics and continued to learn to read, write and do math, though at a slower pace than her age level. Up to this point, she still received speech therapy and physical therapy. They moved her from active physical therapy to being monitored monthly. She also attended two physical education (PE) classes, with one of these being adaptive PE. It was soon after being in placed in first grade that she was dismissed from speech therapy, though at the encouragement of either the teacher or us parents, she could be placed back on the active list if necessary. These were all school related services. Lisa was also involved with the Services for Crippled Children's clinics. In 1985 a law changed the name, and this program is now known as the Medically Handicapped Children's Program. [2]

According to this site, the Medically Handicapped Children's Program (MHCP) provides specialized medical services for families with children with disabilities or ongoing health care needs. Services may include coordination/case management, special medical team evaluations, access to specialized physicians and possible payment of treatment services. Lisa also had some help through the Department of Social Services for a while.

We belonged to several organizations, though we did not search for any groups to belong to in the beginning. Our first contact with any organization was on the day Lisa was born. This was with a Pilot Parent. The Pilot Parent Program organization helped to match a parent of a newborn who had a disability with a parent of similar background, including income, other family members and disability of their child. I was involved with the Pilot Parent Program in many aspects, always willing to help the organization and others. The organization became inactive at some point, as far as meetings go, but we still took referrals as they occurred.

The first support group we joined was the Association for Retarded Citizens. We were able to be with others in similar situations and learn what help was available at the local, state and national levels for our daughter. Since that time, this organization changed its name to 'The Arc', doing away with the word retarded. According to their web site, … "As the words 'retardation' and 'retarded' became pejorative, derogatory and demeaning in usage, the organization changed its name to 'The Arc.' Today, the term 'mental retardation' remains the terminology used in the medical field and referenced in many state and federal laws. However, 'intellectual disability' and 'developmental disability' are making their presence known, and we are doing everything in our power to make sure they're adopted more broadly. We strongly believe the only 'r-word' that should be used when referring to people with intellectual and developmental disabilities is 'Respect.' " [3]

We have been active in the Arc for many years and throughout those years, we volunteered for a variety of positions. My husband was President and I was coordinator of publicity for a while, along with doing the membership, board secretary and the monthly newsletter for The Arc of our local chapter. We joined several others organizations, sometimes to the point of having too many meetings to attend and not being able to spend time at home with the family. We were finally a family, happy and adjusted. We had support from many people to help us come to terms with our situation, to accept Lisa for who she is and to love her as a precious member of our family. We were not alone. The help was there when we needed it.

My relationship with Lisa was and is as a parent to a child and friend to friend. She was a prayer come true, just as I wanted when she was born, a beautiful little girl. The Down syndrome was like an added bonus. After one girl and then two boys in quick succession, I truly wanted a nice, quiet, little girl to cuddle and love. As a parent, I was probably very protective of her, but slowly I learned to overcome this. I tried to do more for her than I should have, but I think it was because it was hard for me to let her be independent, for this meant she was growing up. Besides her having Down Syndrome, she was also my baby and I think we mothers tend to hold on to the last one a little longer. She would be scolded or corrected when she did something wrong, though not nearly as harsh or as often as my other children. The older she got, the more daring she was, which in turn warranted more discipline, which she received as needed.

Lisa is a super neat person, who just would not be Lisa without Down syndrome. I love her for who she is, and all we have with her. She has taught me patience, kindness, and a deeper understanding of what is important or insightful. Lisa has shown others what can be done when there is determination, hard work and commitment. I remember a relative marveling at Lisa when she learned to use a spoon appropriately. This surprised me, for I thought it only normal to think that she could and would do those things. I guess this relative just saw the mental retardation and maybe felt it meant Lisa was doomed, never to learn much of anything and that she would never be normal. I have learned that there is no such thing as "normal" except for the setting on a washing machine. I have learned to give my love unconditionally to my child who has a disability and I profited with love returned 100 times over.

Lisa has brought out the best in my family and myself. She taught us that personal appearances are not important, but it is what's inside that counts. Material goods don't mean the same to me, for what we have one day, we may not have the next. Life is precious and to be enjoyed each day, for it doesn't last.

Lisa has shown me how to be happy, how to take things in stride, to accept what we have and to use it to the best of our ability; to try to be the best and not worry about what others have; to be yourself; to be caring, loving and worry-free. I cannot think of any unpleasant experience with Lisa, unless it was the numerous hospitalizations. One hospital stay was for her heart catherization when she was eight months old, an overnight stay in a strange town and the unknown outcome played havoc on our stress level. We had support of family and friends, which helped a lot. She was also in the hospital at different times for croup and pneumonia. I felt comfortable with the hospital and doctors who were in the same town we lived in and I knew that the doctors knew Lisa and would give her the best care and treatment possible.

Another trying hospitalization was in the summer. Weeks of alternating vomiting and diarrhea, with a marked weight loss, placed her in the hospital for many tests. She was so sick and listless that I feared for her life, especially since the tests kept coming up with no answers. The worst part about this situation was the not knowing. All turned out well, with the help and support of friends, family and specialists.

She has definitely demanded more time of us as parents and we were caught up in everything and anything that had to do with her; especially the meetings. We had three other kids who finally helped us to see what we were doing. We learned to ease up on all the meetings and instead, began to enjoy all our children.

From the time Lisa was born, we took her everywhere. I do not ever remember a time when I was embarrassed because of her Down syndrome. She was Lisa, one of our children, whom we dearly loved. In fact, if anything, we probably took her with us more often, because we were so proud of her and wanted others to see and get to know her.

We knew it was important to go out as a couple also, so we would occasionally get a sitter. Granted, the first few times made me somewhat nervous, but with each sitter and each time we were away, it got easier to leave her with others. Getting a sitter was no problem, but I felt it necessary to let the sitter know ahead of time that she had Down syndrome, what concerns there were and that she was really no different than any of the other children. I really can't remember having any problems with this. I do remember a daycare center (not her regular one she attended) that I was going to send her to for one day of care, but I thought if it worked out, I might enroll her in their program. After hearing several inappropriate and rude questions, I told the lady at the daycare what I thought, and I never considered or recommended that place to anyone. Maybe I was over sensitive, but I felt they were out of line. Because of Lisa, I have learned to go after what I want and what I feel is important, and to speak my mind openly. I have changed because of her.

My husband and I have always been a part of Lisa's education and the IEP process. (Individual Educational Plan) The first year or so was overwhelming and somewhat confusing. We were trying to learn about Lisa, her needs, rights and future. No one ever sat down with us to say, "Hey, you have the right to do or say this, to insist on this or whatever, for Lisa." We have learned by trial and error. We had many conferences, IEPs and updates in the beginning. At school age, there was a yearly review and then three-year re-evaluations were the norm. With each year, we learned a little more, wanted a little more and let our concerns be known a little more. We had several occasions where we had challenged a teacher's statement or suggestion, and I know we did not sign several IEPs until they also included additions that we had asked for. There are parents who hollered louder and longer than we did, but we felt, for the most part, the system and people involved have been good and fair for Lisa's sake. We did not set out to rock the boat, because we knew we would still have to be involved with these people in years to come and wanted no problems between us. We did let teachers and administrative people know our cares and concerns in an acceptable and well-mannered way, which we think was the positive way to approach those difficult situations.

The one change that I was excited to see and which finally happened was the integration of children with disabilities into regular schools and classrooms, namely their own neighborhood school. All children have a right to go to the school closest to them. Why should these children with disabilities be bused all over, even as much as an hour from town to town, when they could attend the school that may be only three or four blocks away. Think of that child and their circumstances. It's a positive approach for all involved and I was glad for the changes that had come about with integration issues. For Lisa to go to the same school as her brothers and sister was a neat and sensible change. She thoroughly loved it.

To be able to attend a regular school and classroom, which helped her to broaden her social skills, was very important in the so called 'outside world'. She had till age twenty-one to perfect her skills, because the law allows schooling up to that age. I wanted Lisa to be able to learn as much of the academics as possible, so her chances of a decent job would be better. I felt when she was an adult, she should be living away from us, either in a group home or likely in her own apartment, with another friend or by herself. I wanted to see her in a junior college if that was an interest of hers and definitely have a job where she could support herself and be self-sufficient. And, in my wishes, I thought, "Who knows, she may also fall in love and get married." Why not? I felt she should be so blessed to know that kind of love. She is a human being and she has feelings, just like us. I would not encourage her having children because of her chances of having a child with Down syndrome, but I would be in favor of some kind of lasting, loving relationship.

In the beginning, we thought of who could care for Lisa. Our old will indicated that one of my family members would care for Lisa and her brothers and sister if something happened to us. A lot has changed over the years and we have since established a trust fund for Lisa and now have her siblings involved in her future care, helping her with her finances and personal needs. I always knew there would be a great future for Lisa. She had the potential to do well and has actually done great things. I wanted her to be able to live on her own and she has, and she is enjoying the freedoms we all have. Having a disability has not changed who Lisa is. She knows that having Down syndrome makes her special, but not different.

Bringing Baby Home

Bringing home a newborn from the hospital should not be a scary thing, unless you're a first time mom who had no siblings and never babysat. I was "none of the above." My early years revolved around babysitting for others as a main source of income. I also had three children of my own before Lisa was born. Taking home a newborn with Down syndrome shouldn't be any different than any other baby, but Lisa also had a heart problem. I was really anxious about the whole thing. I did look forward to being at home, but felt inept at caring for her possible medical needs. What if she turned blue, quit breathing or heaven forbid, her heart stopped? What could I do? What would I do? I can look back now and see how unfounded my questions and concerns were. Lisa turned out to be a perfectly normal baby, in spite of her mother. Well, almost.

I know we stayed an extra day at the hospital, but I can't remember if it was for Lisa or for myself. I know I didn't want to leave her there alone, without me and yet my stay there was to end by day three. They don't have that long of a stay anymore, do they? I remember reading about "drive-through" deliveries, or the stop, drop and go birth stories because of no medical insurance or other extenuating circumstances. Some of the comments were aimed to say "shame on the insurance companies", but I'm sure some of the stories were true. Have a baby, stay 24 hours and then go home. Yikes! I'm glad I got to stay at least three days.

Nevertheless, I did not want to leave Lisa there alone. Two other times I had to leave the hospital without a baby and I just didn't think my heart could take it again. The first time was when I had a baby boy who was stillborn. I had been almost six months pregnant and looked like I was ten months pregnant. I went into early labor and had William Eugene, a child I never got to hold in my arms. The second time was less than a year later, when I gave birth to a healthy, robust, 9 ½ pound baby boy. So, in his case you would think that there would be no reason why we couldn't leave the hospital on the same day. Well, I didn't count on him being jaundice, which is a newborn condition that causes the whites of the eyes and skin color to be yellow. His blood levels were just over the range of acceptable. This medical condition has to do with the spleen and bilirubin and newborns sometimes have this condition temporarily. My son had to stay under some special lights, which aided his body in adjusting the bilirubin to a more normal level. It was a tough day when I had to walk out of that hospital empty-handed, as I had done the year before, even though I knew this baby was alive and well and would be soon be home.

So, when the doctors were still running tests or monitoring Lisa's progress for an extra day, I knew I couldn't leave without her. Besides, I had three other children at home. There's no way I'd get any rest at home! Now that I've mentioned newborn skin color, Lisa wasn't yellow but she managed to turn a dusky grey or blue, usually with crying. We learned later on that this was caused by a VSD, ventricular septal defect, or according to The American Heart Association, it is a hole in the wall separating the two lower chambers of the heart. Normally, the left side of the heart only pumps blood to the body, and the heart's right side only pumps blood to the lungs. In a child with VSD, blood can travel across the hole from the left pumping chamber (left ventricle) to the right pumping chamber (right ventricle) and then out into the lung arteries. [4] When she cried, her skin discoloring intensified, which made it more noticeable. Sometimes only her fingernails or even fingers and toes were this color, while the rest of her was nice and pink. The medical concern was not so much her color; the concern was why did Lisa have the change in her color. All I know is Lisa had people's attention whenever this happened, even from me. Over time, I became accustomed to this anomaly and she seemed to be less affected as she grew older. This could be in part because the opening in her heart was closing a little, allowing less blood to scoot across this open passage.

When we finally came home, I had set up a bassinette in the master bedroom that was on the first floor. The other children had rooms upstairs, only some 24 steps to climb, but who's counting. There was no way I wanted Lisa up there, for several reasons. First of all, physically I did not need to make that trip up and down those stairs if I could avoid it; at least for a while. Secondly, I knew I wouldn't feel comfortable if I couldn't check on Lisa constantly, whether she was sleeping or awake. And thirdly, I just had to have her close at hand.

The large bassinette fit just fine in between two dressers and she had more than enough room in it to be comfortable. In fact, she stayed in that bassinette for almost three months without outgrowing it. (Unlike her hefty, 9 ½ pound brother, born almost three years earlier, who kept bumping his head at the head of the bassinette on day two of his life.) Having Lisa nearby helped my anxiety level, though it gave me more opportunities to check on her. This was probably NOT good. Naturally, I would go check on her and lift her out if and when she whimpered. She never really cried much, but I'm wondering if it's because I never gave her a chance to cry. The littlest peep had me at her side, checking for the cause of her slightest possible discomfort. Her crying was very quiet and unconvincing to most people. But I was almost paranoid with the idea of keeping her stress-free, so I overreacted to any noise she made. She cooed a lot in her sleep and made other wonderful baby noises. I just knew this meant she would be a talker. (She did talk fairly early and pretty clearly, but I don't know if there's any scientific testing to prove early noises means early talking.) Her soft, little noises brought me to her side, to look at her in wonder, hoping and praying her future would be good.

I was also drawn to her side when she didn't make any noise. At first, she probably didn't get any rest, because I would check on her hourly plus any other time I thought she should be awake but wasn't. I would go into the room, but never trying to be quiet and never tiptoeing. I learned with my other children that if you try to be quiet around a baby, they would never learn to sleep with noise and there's no way to keep a perfectly quiet house during nap time, especially when there are other children in the house or in the neighborhood for that matter. I remember with my first baby, I would get mad at the outside noise, like car horns honking, loud trucks, trains or someone mowing the lawn. And you know there's no way to quiet those things. So, to acclimate a baby to noise is a good thing, for the baby and the parents.

Now, I would get close to Lisa's bassinette and do my look, listen and feel maneuvers. First, I'd watch to see if the blankets moved with each inhalation and expiration. This was easily done when a blanket was draped across her, but more difficult to detect if the angle of view was wrong or there were too many covers. Next step would be to listen. This is a given, regardless of if I had determined her respirations or not. I always had to listen. If she were sleeping peacefully, she would coo and make those other cutesy noises. So, I'd stay awhile and listen. If she had congestion, she usually sounded wheezy or noisy and you could definitely hear her from about anywhere on the first floor of our house. (It was a small house!) Of course, I'd have to check to make sure nothing else was obstructing her breathing. The third step would be to feel for her breathing pattern, especially when I wasn't one hundred percent sure the first two ways gave me the accurate and reassuring findings I needed. Now, I didn't just feel her chest or back area on top of the covers, but I'd gently slip my fingers through the layers of blankets and clothing to feel her skin for warmth, as well as movement. And I didn't just check there. The nose and mouth released warm air, which was easily felt. If up to this point I still wasn't convinced of her breathing properly or at all, this technique of holding a finger near her nose and/or mouth did convince me. I always thought there could be a brochure on one hundred different ways to check your child's breathing. I believe I just covered a few.

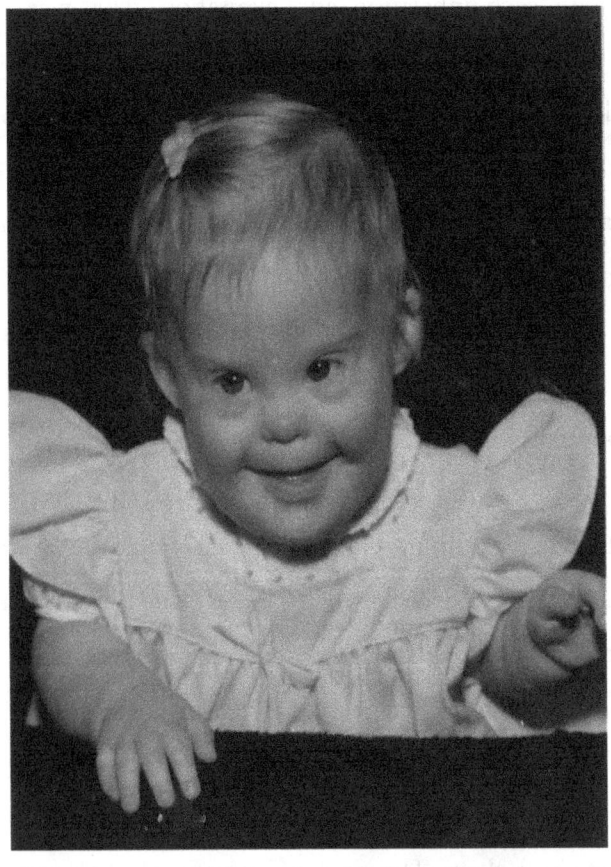

Acceptance

There is no set time or incidence when a parent who has a child with a disability can say, "Okay, I accept this, I will do anything I can to make it the best situation possible." When you are told in the delivery room that your child isn't perfect, it feels like someone unexpectedly pulled the floor out from under you and you are now falling one hundred miles an hour, down, down, down. I cannot imagine that anyone who hears the words, "Your child has Down syndrome" or cerebral palsy, or having a missing limb, or anything out of the ordinary, could immediately say "Hey, that's great. It's more than I had hoped for," or "That's just what I wanted for my child."

If there are circumstances or parents like that, God bless you. You must be able to adjust and accept surprises better than I do. I have a nephew who, when he heard about Lisa, actually sounded pleased. He had experienced a wonderful relationship with his Dad's sister, who had Down syndrome. He just thought it was a great thing to now have a cousin like that, which to him must have meant having fun with his cousin. He saw the disability as an asset to someone's personality, where as I initially saw it as a negative quality. I must admit I struggled with Lisa's diagnosis. I tried to deny it and wondered why such a thing could happen to her, and yes, to us. I saw all the signs that identified the disability, but rationalized why it couldn't possibly be Down syndrome. I would not accept the obvious, and I tried to deny there could be anything wrong with her. I was going to make MY final diagnosis after the hip x-rays and chromosome tests came back. Until that happened, I still hoped that the Down syndrome wasn't there. So I would closely watch her for any such sign that could reassure me that she didn't have the syndrome. Lisa didn't give me much to work with.

She was a very good baby, very quiet and easily satisfied. She slept or at least pretended to sleep during the breast feedings. She just wasn't interested in eating or getting to know the world around her. Nothing I did would wake her. I tickled her feet, patted them, tweaked her toes, rubbed the top of her head, undressed her, patted her cheeks; everything. The word used to describe Lisa would be lethargic. She didn't respond to any stimuli, which was one of the categories on the Apgar score test that was done at birth. Obviously, she didn't pass it then and even after being in the world for three whole days she didn't respond much. This should have been a clue for me.

And, if I had gotten her to wake up and open her eyes, I would have seen grey spots around the outer edge of the iris, named Brushfield's spots. [5] According to Wikipedia.org, they are small, white or grayish/brown spots on the periphery of the iris in the human eye due to aggregation of connective tissue, a normal iris element. I don't notice them so much now, but when she was a baby, they were definitely discernable. (If she ever opened her eyes, which she rarely did as newborn.) She also had a simian line, another typical characteristic, though not all people with Down syndrome have this. And, some people who don't have Down syndrome have this single, palmer crease, so you just never know with this telltale sign.

She was able to lift her head up off the hospital bassinette mattress, struggling to hold that wobbly head. And I would silently convince myself that she couldn't possibly have Down syndrome, thinking, "Look at how strong she is already. She can hold her head up." And then I'd cry, because deep inside, I knew that she probably did have Down syndrome.

Her body size was somewhat larger than normal for a newborn, tipping the scales at eight pounds, thirteen ounces at birth; larger than two of my three other children. Even the doctor, before telling us his suspicions in the delivery room, had to ask how much our other children weighed, for comparison. Many children who have Down syndrome have a smaller birth weight, but not Lisa. This fact just continued to reinforce my belief that the doctors must be wrong in their early diagnosis of Lisa. I couldn't imagine someone as innocent and helpless as her or any newborn, could have Down syndrome. But then I thought, where did all the adults with Down syndrome come from if not first as a baby. Now remember, you are not dealing with thoughts from a rational person, especially in those early days after Lisa's birth and I was a mom who wanted the best for her child. At that time, to me, wanting the best for Lisa did NOT include her having Down syndrome.

I finally saw the proof in black and white, when the chromosome report came back. It's funny, but you'd think as obsessive as I was about "knowing for sure" whether she had Down syndrome, that I would remember where I was when I finally received the news. I seem to recall receiving a letter, but I think that this should have been something the doctor would have sat down and discussed with us in detail. And he probably had already done that when we were still in the hospital, ending his talk with "Take her home and love her." But then, six weeks after the blood was drawn, there it was, black on white, with a lot of blots that looked like squished bugs, all lined up in pairs, all marked and identified; all except for the 21st chromosome notation. There were 3 splotches. They glared at me as if to say, "Now do you believe it?" Still in denial, I thought "Of course not, because I had read somewhere that these tests aren't one hundred percent accurate." That's when I had to say "Whoa, I think I need some help!"

During all this time, I was still her mom, I still loved her dearly and worked with her every chance I could. I was not in denial as far as not doing anything. I wasn't going to take a chance that if she *did* have Down syndrome and I hadn't been working to help her in every way possible, that my lack of trying to help Lisa would just delay her success. So, most of my uncertainty and wishful thinking was kept inside, except in prayer, which may have been considered pleading at the time.

Now I can look back and see how silly I was, how absolutely ridiculous it was for me to spend all that time in denial when it was so obvious. It was really only a few days for me to come to terms with her having Down syndrome, but the chromosome results gave me closure. I could finally know and can accept that Lisa would not be

Lisa without the Down syndrome; that is a part of who she was and is, irreplaceable in this world. And I love her unconditionally, not wanting to change any thing about her. I am only human and at first I couldn't come to terms with the plateful I was handed. I had to deal with it in my own way and time. I wish I could have said, "I don't mind Lisa having Down syndrome" when she was born, but it just didn't happen like that, at least not for me. There was a point in time when I no longer thought about it daily, as I had in those first few days after her birth. And then, when I had become comfortable with it, I still felt like I was waiting for the other shoe to drop. I know other parents said they rode the same roller coaster I had, until some milestone event happened. These other parents of children with Down syndrome said you suddenly see your child again, and realize that they still have Down syndrome and will never be that "average, typical" child you thought you had. Then, you move on.

I believe this happened for me during a devastating and overwhelming IEP [6] (Individual Educational Plan) meeting, where it was decided that the things I wanted for Lisa were just not possible. That was when I saw Lisa differently. Not in a bad way, but still with a feeling that I'd lost who I thought she was. She was and still is Lisa. At that moment I thought, "She can still become an adult ready to meet the world head on, to be independent, have her own place, work at a job, buy her own groceries and be a contributing member in society." I watched her with all her trials and accomplishments, how hard she had worked and how much she had succeeded and I wondered why. Not "why did it happen", but "why did I wonder?"

Welcome To Holland

It was a busy place at the hospital when Lisa was born and there were visits from doctors, nurses, priest, chaplain, friends and family. Our hospital stay was definitely not a quiet one. I was busy coping with the news of Lisa having Down syndrome; Lisa kept busy turning grey and dusky blue. I was busy trying to breastfeed; Lisa was trying to sleep through it. I was busy worrying about what to do if, once we were home, I was holding her and she quit breathing or if I went to check her bed and she had quit breathing or if I was changing her dirty diaper and she quit breathing. I remember thinking "What would I do if these things happened?" You can see a pattern here, can't you? I worried about everything, but at this early point in time, my worry was most focused her breathing. Other nonsensical questions were thoughts like how do I hold her, how do I bottle feed her, how do I dress and care for her every need? You'd have thought I never had a baby before.

I know I was having trouble mentally and emotionally, trying to accept news of the Down syndrome and then as quickly, a heart problem. It was just so new and I was not very knowledgeable in this area. The word that comes to mind is ignorant. Not that I was dumb or stupid, but simply ignorant. I just hadn't been exposed to this information until she was born, so really, how was I to know. This was also how I looked at it later on, when others would eventually come in contact with Lisa. Those people really didn't know much either, until they had the experience of being around a person with a disability. Nevertheless, in the first few days and weeks, those who came to wish us well did not always get that learning time with Lisa and I was quick to judge their remarks as off-handed, rude and maybe even stupid.

The worst comments were in connection with the never-ending pedestal some people wanted to put us on as parents of a child with a developmental disability. "You must be special parents to have someone like Lisa." "God knew you could handle it, so he gave you Lisa." "You must be blessed." Well, I do feel blessed, only because God has given us four children to raise and enjoy. But, I don't believe God is sitting on his golden throne on a fluffy cloud in heaven, deciding who should have a child with a disability. I believe he allows this to happen, to help us to grow, to learn and experience all that we can during our time on earth and to grow in love for our children and for those who may be considered different. I do not blame God for Lisa's Down syndrome, because scientifically I know it was an error during the early stages of embryo development. And we are not special parents; just parents who choose to have and raise children.

Those comments by others were intended to be of comfort to us, I'm sure or maybe they just didn't know what else to say. People had trouble congratulating us on having another baby. Part of that could be because we already had three children under the age of eight. Others probably wondered how we could be happy with a newborn that wasn't picture-perfect. So they couldn't say the usual remarks like, "She's so pretty, cute or beautiful" or "She looks just like you, Dad or Grandma." And the cards that came were more generic. There were very few of those cute cards that gush over the ten fingers and toes or perfect little angel themes. I can look back now and see the dilemma others were in and I can understand their hesitation in congratulations because I was also confused as to how I should feel and act. That has changed and so have I. Having a child with a disability may seem like a misfortune in the beginning, but that feeling changes with time. It's like preparing for a trip. Emily Perl Kingsley said it best in a poem entitled "A trip to Holland."

Welcome To Holland

By

Emily Perl Kingsley

© 1987 by Emily Perl Kingsley

All rights reserved   Reprinted by permission of the author

I am often asked to describe the experience of raising a child with a disability - to try to help people who have not shared that unique experience to understand it, to imagine how it would feel. It's like this…

BARCUS

When you're going to have a baby, it's like planning a fabulous vacation trip - to Italy. You buy a bunch of guide books and make your wonderful plans. The Coliseum. The Michelangelo David. The gondolas in Venice. You may learn some handy phrases in Italian. It's all very exciting.

After months of eager anticipation, the day finally arrives. You pack your bags and off you go. Several hours later, the plane lands. The flight attendant comes in and says, "Welcome to Holland."

"Holland?!?" you say. "What do you mean Holland?? I signed up for Italy! I'm supposed to be in Italy. All my life I've dreamed of going to Italy."

But there's been a change in the flight plan. They've landed in Holland and there you must stay.

The important thing is that they haven't taken you to a horrible, disgusting, filthy place, full of pestilence, famine and disease. It's just a different place.

So you must go out and buy new guide books. And you must learn a whole new language. And you will meet a whole new group of people you would never have met.

LOVING AND LEARNING

It's just a <u>different</u> place. It's slower-paced than Italy, less flashy than Italy. But after you've been there for a while and you catch your breath, you look around…and you begin to notice that Holland has windmills…and Holland has tulips. Holland even has Rembrandts.

But everyone you know is busy coming and going from Italy…and they're all bragging about what a wonderful time they had there. And for the rest of your life, you will say, "Yes, that's where I was supposed to go. That's what I had planned."

And the pain of that will never, ever, ever, ever go away…because the loss of that dream is a very, very significant loss.

But…if you spend your life mourning the fact that you didn't get to Italy, you may never be free to enjoy the very special, the very lovely things…about Holland.

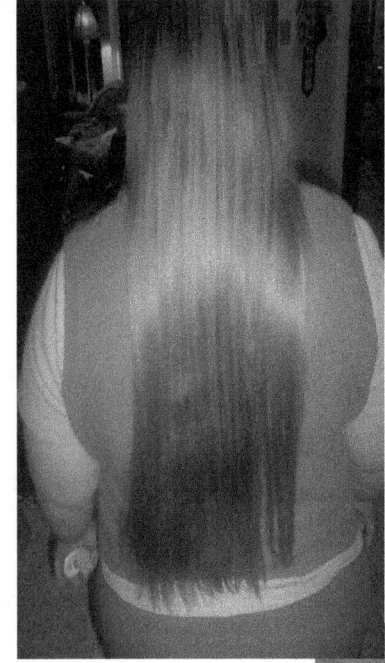

Dad's Hair-dos For Lisa

In the early '80s, I was a mom and a housewife. With four small children at home, it was probably an obvious career choice. I enjoyed being home with the kids, besides being in on all the other activities that go along with being a mom and a housewife. I helped with the PTA, grade level room mom, made treats, sewed costumes, volunteered at school and church, had a weekly bowling day out, was a taxi driver to anything and everything and whatever else there was to do. Now, I did have lots of help from my husband, but he was the chief breadwinner and I respected his position and hard work. There was a definite attitude change in both of us when I decided to go to school in order to obtain an education in some field of study. By doing so, I would have better work choices that would give me more options if I ever needed to hold a job outside of being a stay-at-home mom.

By this time all the kids were in school, which was a prerequisite for me before I committed a year to a higher education. There was the task of coordinating rides to and from the kids' schools and daycare facilities and at times that was pretty tricky. Thank goodness my husband worked in or close to town and was available whenever there was a glitch in the plan. I don't believe he realized the commitment he also made when he agreed that I should go back to school and get some higher education experience.

One of the biggest challenges for him was Lisa's hair. I used to do all sorts of braids and styles, pulling back all of it in a ponytail, doing pigtails on the sides and other ways using rubber bands and plastic hair clips. He learned the very basic "tail", one large ponytail at the back of her head. Sometimes it would be high, sometimes low and close to the nape of her neck. Sometimes Lisa wanted to have it way off to one side, showing just how fashionable she could be. Or, this style could have been the result of Lisa turning her head to one side while Dad was trying to put the ponytail in and consequently the end result was off to one side. He may have tried pigtails on both sides, but that takes a little more work, making sure they are even in the amount of hair and in placement for each pigtail.

Barrettes were always used to keep those loose hairs out of her face but those also took some manipulating. I would also try to make a straight part when dividing Lisa's hair, but my husband's lines weren't entirely straight. I'm not complaining, I'm just stating the differences in our techniques. (I was so lucky to have him there in the mornings to get Lisa ready and off to school because I had to leave the house rather early to catch a ride with another student. And we had to drive about 40 minutes, so the earlier the better, especially in inclement weather.) But, with my husband now having to do the morning hair routine, I felt like I had to let go of something that had been my job for many years and I did not turn this over to him easily. I tried to set out different barrettes that would match her clothes. I did continue to pick out her clothes the night before because who knows what kind of clothes would be matched for her if I didn't do that. I couldn't give up all my control all at once.

Besides putting the hair in the standard ponytail, he had to comb it, which was sometimes a real struggle. Lisa's scalp must have been super tender, because using certain combs and brushes made her very unhappy. Of course, some of that could have been because of all the rats or tangles she acquired throughout the night. Lisa's hair was long and very fine in texture.

If I let it down loose for her to sleep, it was really a mess by the morning. If I tried to keep the hair pulled back, she had trouble sleeping on the "bump." So, either way it was a problem. Most of the time it was loose at night, so combing her hair every morning was not a happy, fun time. There was a trick to it, which I passed along to my husband when he took over. If you started at the bottom ends, far from her scalp and combed that first, I learned that worked the best.

Gradually, you could move up towards the hair shaft, closer to the scalp with each round. When there was a tangled area, it took a little more time and patience. Pulling on it hard only increased the complaints of discomfort. At times, I had thoughts of using a scissors and getting rid of that tangled web easily. But that would only make things look worse, with the tangles cut away and bald spots all over. I do remember some troubles with the rubber bands being left in all-night and becoming so tangled in the hair that the rubber bands had to be cut away. That meant some hair was lost as well, but not entire lengths of hair.

Lisa's Dad took over as Mr. Mom for that year, doing more than his share of things I used to do before I started school. It was good for him and me, but I really think Lisa also benefitted as well because she became closer to her Dad, actually wanting to go with him and do things that I probably wouldn't have thought that she would like to do. She said she liked fixing wires such as the television cable line and working on cars. This she did not get from me. She must have been watching her Dad. She liked working in the garden with him and running to the hardware store. Again, not from me. And yes, it was nice to have Dad as a backup caregiver and not always having the family expect mom to clean the house, do the everyday errands or make supper.

Supper was always a fun experience when Lisa and her Dad got near the spices. So it was a good experience for all of us, having Dad in a different role. What started out as a necessity, turned into positive out-comes. I was able to let go of some of what I thought were my duties as a mom and housewife, to step out of the typical stereotype role I had assumed early in our marriage. My husband stepped in, took over some duties some Dads didn't normally do and the bond was formed between Dad and daughter. It was a win-win situation for all of us.

Hospital Stay

Lisa's hospital visits had been few in number and did not usually last more than a few hours. (This is the magic of outpatient surgery; one example: to insert tubes in the ears.) There was one experience in the hospital that lasted a week, with lots of new and exciting things for Lisa to learn about. Being in the hospital is no fun for anyone, but for a child it is actually scary and uncertain. Lisa's first night, neither she nor I slept much. Yes, I stayed the night with Lisa, because I couldn't leave her there alone, especially since she seemed scared. She didn't feel well, which didn't help the situation. If she had felt fine, we wouldn't be there in the first place. Everyone there was a stranger except me. She was leery of the nurses doing anything, whether it was taking her temperature, blood pressure or to have blood drawn. Ouch! The procedures were explained to her but she wasn't convinced it would be to her benefit. An oral temp should have been easy to do, but when mom always took her temperature under the arm, sticking that thing in her mouth may have seemed really weird to her.

I volunteered to have my temperature taken, repeating the procedure as many times as the nurses came in to take Lisa's temperature, reassuring Lisa that it didn't hurt and it would be over real fast. (I also found out my temp was normal on those days.) It took lots of talking to finally get her to cooperate. One time she was half asleep, so just suggesting she open her mouth was all it took. That was so much easier but that was short lived. When she was awake, her dolls Miss Molly Dolly and Mr. Bob Balloon had their temperatures taken before Lisa. Sleep was not in the plans for us, though I had good intentions when I adjusted the chair to a makeshift bed. Pulling the footstool out was easy, flipping the cushion down was easy, reading the directions to lower the headrest was easy; but that's when things got tough. I must have been a weakling because I could not "Gently push footrest forward, at the same time you pull the lever up to release." A strong nurse came to my rescue.

    A pillow and blanket were provided. We had all the comforts of home. But, Lisa was so restless that everything bothered her. She had wanted to sleep on the floor because the bed was not hers. Those strange rails on the sides really bothered her at first and when I put up the lower rails on either side at the foot of the bed, you'd have thought she was claustrophobic. She also had trouble wearing the hospital gown and asked over and over to wear her own pajamas. Finally, I had Lisa put on her pajamas one night and she was happy to have her own colorfully, animal-print feet pajamas. They worked great at nighttime when all she had to do was sleep, but during the day, for convenience reasons for the nurses, she was in the gown.

    To comfort and reassure her, I decided to show her the bed was really okay. I crawled into bed with her, having her scoot over a little and I told her to "please share your pillow." She finally settled down and soon drifted off to a light sleep. When I tried to move my position, her heavy eyelids would open ever so slightly, just to make sure I was still there. I finally did manage to get out but felt like I was in combat training; slowly crawling over the rails, then dropping to the floor and trying to do it all quietly. Did you ever notice that most hospital beds have a squeak somewhere?

This was now the time for a trip to the bathroom for me, since I could not get away while Lisa was awake. A couple of times I tried to leave her bedside when she was still wide-awake. While I was out of the room, Lisa would push the Nurse Button because she wanted lotion on her hands or some other such reason. It did not take her long to figure out the buttons that work the call system, lights and the bed. I had to discourage her use of the buttons as she got better each day or I would discover that she ordered mashed potatoes again for her snack.

We knew she was getting better because she started eating anything and everything. Broccoli and cauliflower were never her choice of foods voluntarily, but when her appetite came back, she welcomed those foods as if she had always loved the taste. Her favorite food choice was mashed potatoes and she ordered it for every meal, yes, even breakfast. And she always got what she ordered.

About day two of her one-week stay, the nurses were trying to get her ready for a radiology exam and Lisa was to have the chalky, white barium drink. She refused to have any part of the drink in her room, so they said the drink could be given in the radiology department. I went along to help because I was sure this would not go over well. They filled a squirt bottle with the unappealing drink and told Lisa to take a squirt and swallow. This did not happen. So, I tried to give her a squirt but she quickly clamped her mouth shut and turned her head swiftly. Immediately, most of the white, chalky liquid flowed down the side of her mouth and down the front of her gown. Lisa and I came to a standoff, so I talked to her about the importance of this medicine helping the doctor to find out what was wrong. I remember that she did take some of the drink, gagging with each swallow, but willing herself to gulp it down just the same. I don't think the results of the tests were conclusive, as the prep amount probably wasn't sufficient to reveal the medical problem. The closest we came to getting a diagnosis was suspected giardia infection. This is a common waterborne disease and found in swimming pools and water fountains. She had been at the pool and probably drinking the water from both the fountains AND the pool.

  I knew she was ready to go home when she got tired of being in the bed all the time, and when she started playing her own "bed" games, jumping up and down to see what toys and dolls could be knocked off the side rails. Yup, time to go home!

LOVING AND LEARNING

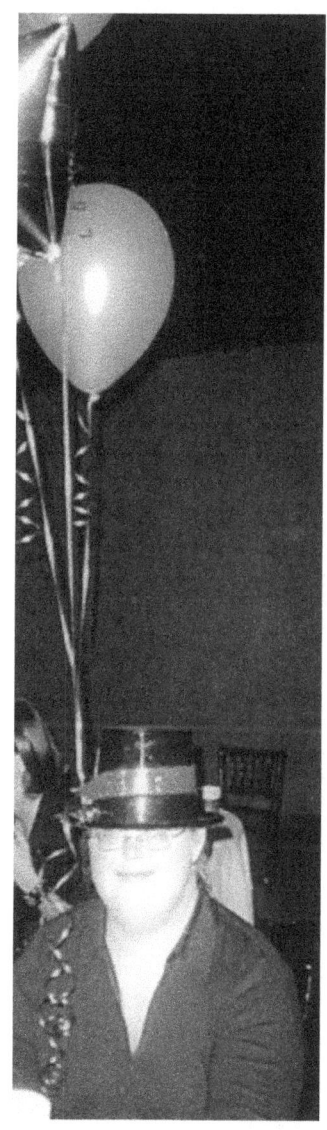

BARCUS

Discipline: A Challenge

I use to let Lisa crawl up on the coffee table, just to see if she could get up there. I used to let her use her fingers to eat, just to see her feed herself. But, at some point I had to say 'no more'. Her antics and actions at 3 ½ told me that she would accomplish more in her lifetime than I had ever imagined. So, at an early age, I knew I needed to exert a little discipline and appropriate punishment when she challenged our parenting ways.

My first hint that some changes were needed came from our other children. On occasion, there would be a slight comment from a sibling saying something like, "Mom, you would never let me get away with that." The real awakening was when I got upset and inadvertently blamed one of the other children for something Lisa had done. The most difficult thing for me was in being stern with her. After all, she did have a disability. I soon realized that was not a reason or an excuse for her to get away with things; she was more normal than not, so I changed my ways, and discipline was then not as difficult as I had imagined. When she went to the cupboard and drug out the various sizes of cans of food to stack and roll around on the kitchen floor, she was also made to put them away afterwards. She usually complied with this directive but only after a lot of reminding. When she played with an item that should not be touched, such as a statue or some other precious piece, she was corrected. I don't remember that I ever spanked her but I might have swatted her hands if she had done something that could have injured her self or others. And then, my action was more of a reaction to what Lisa was about to do that could be harmful. One time she wanted to help cook, so she reached for the hot pan on the stove. I quickly grabbed her hand and moved her swiftly away from the danger. Those ever present and always noticeable electrical outlets were also a real temptation when she was near them. So, another swift action on my part to remove her from the temptation was my best defense to keep her safe. Once she started walking instead of crawling by the low outlets, that temptation seemed to be 'out of sight, out of mind'.

She was disciplined during eating times, church times and social times. She needed direction and that's what I tried to do. She needed to know right from wrong. To grow up without discipline would not benefit her or others. Disciplining her was a challenge, but then so was she. As she grew older, many new situations came about that made me stop and think about if, how or why I might discipline Lisa. It was a never-ending challenge. I would never call her negative actions behavior problems but I was mindful of what they were and why she might be acting out in a certain way. There were times when Lisa would just ignore me when I was trying to redirect her actions into something positive. I wondered if she could hear me or was she just ignoring me. Kids seem to turn off their hearing at will and sometimes at inappropriate times. I might have told Lisa that she needed to get dressed for church, only to find out ten minutes later that she was still watching television. So, did she hear me or ignore me? I learned to get eye contact before saying something and then she would usually complete the request I had made. Later on, we discovered she did indeed have some hearing issues, probably due to the numerous ear infections she had over the early years. From the website, the National Down Syndrome Society [7] (NDSS) the most common medical problems that may be associated with behavior changes include vision or hearing deficits, thyroid function, sleep apnea, depression and several other such health issues.

The National Down Syndrome Society also relates some of the common behavior concerns there are for children with Down syndrome such as wandering or running off, stubborn or oppositional behavior and attention problems, to name a few. I can relate Lisa's antics or her negative behavior problems to those that I mentioned but I don't believe I would consider them as behavior issues. Maybe I gave her too much leeway, but I believed it was her way of testing her limits, wanting to be independent and trying to become more responsible in her actions. Let's look at her wandering and running off. Well, she didn't ever run away from home, but she did start riding a bicycle and that caused some issues. The first time she ventured away from the house much further than I felt comfortable with, I found her down the street and around the corner out of my line of vision. I lifted her and her bicycle up, turned her around and pointed the way home, using my gruff voice to let her know that she had gone to far away from home. She never did that again, at least as far as I knew. I tried to give her space to explore and grow, but within my limits.

Now, about being stubborn or oppositional. Yes, she was and still is, on occasion. I believe when she was still in the homebound program [8] she was too young to realize that she was being stubborn. Sometimes she wouldn't open her mouth when we tried to place peanut butter on the inside of her mouth, to encourage tongue exercises. Well, maybe she was not hungry at that time, so refusing it seemed to be a reasonable reaction. Maybe she didn't like peanut butter that day. Maybe she was just tired of her tongue exercises. Who knows? In grade school, she would shut down during a challenging situation. More specifically, when doing math problems. If she was pushed to far, or made to work through something that she thought was too difficult, she would just shut down and refuse to do anything. We, the teacher and I, came up with ways to work around her attitude, getting her to finish the work and that she could still feel like a happy camper about the situation. Did we let her win the battle of the minds? Maybe. But did she learn something from it. Probably. Did she grow up and exhibit more stubbornness? No. The key word is 'more'. She has and probably always will be stubborn, but I never considered it a problematic behavioral concern. Others may say differently.

In regards to Lisa's attention problems, I will reiterate that her hearing issues, and most likely her vision problems, may have been a contributing factor to her attention problems. What we did while she was in school was to be sure the teachers knew about her hearing and vision concerns and we requested preferential seating to optimize her learning. Her listening skills are better, so we haven't had to check her hearing in quite awhile. Lisa has always had and still receives yearly vision checks, to follow any changes that might occur in a year's time. So, when it comes to attention problems or issues, there are several additional points to be aware of. Is there a medical problem or emotional stressors that might be a contributing factor? The National Down Syndrome Society (NDSS) [9] website states: "Work with a professional (psychologist, behavioral pediatrician, counselor) to develop a behavior treatment plan using the ABC's of behavior. (Antecedent, Behavior, Consequence of the behavior)." And lastly, medication might be necessary, especially in situations where the child has Attention Deficit Hyperactivity Disorder (ADHD) or autism.

On one of Lisa's first time-outs in the corner, she had to sit on a small brown rocking chair, be quiet and think about what caused the current misbehavior. I quickly learned I had made a rookie mistake. Placing her in her favorite chair for television watching was the wrong move. Move is the key word because that was what she would do, move her chair by rocking. But, I only made that mistake once. I also tried to have her go to time out on the bottom step of the stairs that led to the second floor. She sat there quietly, so I thought that the placement was a good choice. I had also read somewhere that the rule of thumb for children if they are given a time-out punishment was for every year of their age, they could sit for one minute. So, when she was four she should be able to sit for four minutes. I don't believe she had time-outs at age four, but I do remember at a young age, I had Lisa sitting on that bottom step. It was carpeted and had a fairly wide staircase. I walked away while she was contemplating her "action" and I went about some quick household chores. I am sure I wasn't out of the room more than a minute, but when I returned to see if she was still sitting there, I had to giggle at the site. Lisa had taken off her shoes, curled up on her left side, facing away from the stair step she was on, and she was sleeping. Well, was that punishment or was that her being creative in her discipline situation and deciding it was just the right time to take a nap. Lisa did not need a lot of discipline, because she was fairly even tempered, mild mannered and did behave well most of the time. Those iffy situations were few and far between, so I dealt with them rather quickly and hopefully fairly. With any luck, the discipline was fair for whatever misdeed Lisa may have committed.

I am sure there are different opinions about discipline, such as what is correct or good for the child. I am the first to admit I sometimes probably did it wrong, but I tried to do the best I could. I love my children, and want them to have lots of love from me, but I knew I had to also be the parent, and discipline is part of what it takes to parent. I wanted my children to know right from wrong and tried to be consistent in my ways.

I let them know that I was in charge and that even though I would discipline them, I would also always love them. I don't know how my early years may have influenced my discipline techniques, but I feel that it had some bearing on how I disciplined my children. They are all adults now and they all turned out okay, as far as I know. I believe we all try to do the best we can under the circumstances when it comes to discipline.

Years ago, I came across a one-page photocopy of an article in the Down Syndrome News, May 1992 newsletter. It opened my eyes to what we say and what we do, and how we shape things to suit our needs.

Double Standards of Labeling

If an adult is reinforced for behaving appropriately, we call it recognition.

If a child is reinforced for behaving appropriately, we call it bribery.

If an adult writes in a book, we call it doodling.

If a child writes in a book, we call it destroying property.

If an adult sticks to something, we call it perseverance.

If a child sticks to something, we call it stubbornness.

If an adult seeks help, we call it consulting.

If a child seeks help, we call it whining.

If an adult is not paying attention, we call it preoccupation.

If a child is not paying attention, we call it distractibility.

If an adult tells his side of the story, we call it clarification.

If a child tells his side of the story, we call it talking back.

If an adult raises his voice in anger, we call it maintaining control.

If a child raises his voice in anger, we call it a temper tantrum.

If an adult hits a child, we call it discipline.

If a child hits a child, we call it fighting.

If an adult behaves in an unusual way, we call it unique.

If a child behaves in an unusual way, we refer him for a psychological evaluation.

(From "Parent to Parent," newsletter of MPACT as adapted from an article by Dixie Fletcher, printed in Education Update)

Summer Plans

Summer was fast approaching and I wasn't sure I was ready. Lisa was four and attending a center-based preschool program. This year would be a little different, but not because of the program she would attend. Lisa would go to the center-based summer school program as in the past but now, instead of Lisa getting on a bus every morning, I decided I wanted to drive her to and from school. I had opted not to use the bus service in order to take her to her classes myself. I wanted to be more involved and to know what she was doing every day. What it boiled down to was that I would do more driving and I silently thought, is it worth it? Speaking for myself, yes. I had the same attitude with Lisa and her needs as I had with her siblings. Their summer activities kept them busy, which made me happy. Besides the recreational entertainment, summer was a time that they would also improve their athletic skills, be it in swimming, tennis, softball or whatever. It was well worth my time to give them the opportunity to grow, in whatever they tried. So it would be with Lisa, too. Her schooling was important, be it during the school year or during summer school program. We should all be grateful for the dedicated teachers who were willing to teach through the summer months. Lisa's teachers, as well as my husband and I, felt Lisa needed year-round stimulation, so with summer school, she had a chance for continued improvement. Without it, she may have become stagnant or even reverted in some areas. So we were very fortunate to have our summer sessions, our school system and the special teachers involved.

To me, summer meant two and a half months of coping with my kids, day in and day out. What was I thinking? HELP! No, not really, but thank goodness for their varied activities. This kept them busy even though that meant I was also busy driving them all over town. But that was ok, because I could work it around my summer school nursing job. Besides school for Lisa that summer, I wanted to also involve her in other social activities. The public library had weekly filmstrips geared for children as well as a story hour of some sort. I even thought that if our summer visits to the library went well, we might consider continuing this activity in the fall. I believe a love of books never hurt anyone. If I start a book that truly captures my attention, you may as well forget the house cleaning, clothes getting washed or early dinner, though I've been known to cook or vacuum with a book in one hand!

Other outside activities included trips to the YMCA for swim lessons or open swimming. There was even a day camp for our children with developmental disabilities. I know lots of parents took advantage of that program, in addition to the summer school classes. There were many opportunities available and it was just a matter of checking out the information to see what we wanted Lisa and her siblings involved in during those 8-12 weeks between the end of the school and the beginning of the fall school session. I did look forward to summer no matter how hectic some days were. There were also lazy days in the sun, long evenings on the porch swing and best of all---no snow. How did I get ready? I got tennis shoes for those daily walks and bike rides, shorts for the warm days ahead and most definitely, a full tank of gas for all those trips around town.

Lisa's center-based summer program was fun. I think Lisa even enjoyed it. I loved the variety and less structured schedules. When the teachers brought the sand table outside, the children would squeal with delight. They knew that this waist-high table would be more fun outside, because they wouldn't be told to keep the sand in the divided table. They could fling sand around, try to build a castle, a road or a mountain and not worry about the ground getting full of sand. The downside was when they ran out of sand. Then, the teachers would change the sand table into a water table and the squeals became louder shrieks, with the anticipation of a lot of water fun. This would usually be on a day where the teachers asked for swimsuits, towels and maybe even an extra change of clothes. Lisa wasn't into swimming so much, but that was probably my fault. I was concerned with recurrent ear infections, so I kept her water activities to bathtubs and back yard plastic pools. But, she loved the water table and it was nowhere close to her ears, so she could delight in the splashing, dipping and throwing of water; on everyone. And invariably, the end would come about when their scheduled time was over or when they ran out of water. So, that summer I was able to spend time driving my children to the many summer activities they had and I enjoyed watching them as they played hard and fast. The summers didn't last long, but it was always a nice change for all of us.

BARCUS

Loosening The Tight Apron Strings

How soon is too soon to loosen the apron strings? I felt the tugs begin when Lisa was seven and I tried desperately to tie those strings in knots! Is age seven too young to let go? I guess it depended on what Lisa wanted to do. My thoughts on her independence began when I started to see that Lisa was filled with many self-determining ideas that made me stop and realize she was growing up, with or without my consent.

I did veto the walk to the park alone, for many reasons. I thought four blocks in Grandma's town was a little too much for her to tackle alone. At least that's what I thought in the beginning. What I did do on one occasion was walk with her, showing her landmarks in the hopes that it would help her to remember where to turn, so she could get back to Grandma's house. Then I allowed her to "walk on her own", with me following. I let her make her own decisions as to where to turn but adjusted her course when we ended up going the wrong way. I remember my own venture when our family moved from a farmhouse to a house in town. I was about 8, and on my first bicycle ride down a couple of blocks from home I got lost. I didn't even turn any corners. I just didn't realize that all I had to do was turn around and go back the way I came, hopefully ending up at the new house where we had just moved.

Finally came the day when I let Lisa try to go on a walk alone, and unbeknownst to her, I was quietly following her. As it happened, she never did make it to the park, for the neighbor's swing set was beckoning her silently with its shiny red paint and the slightly moving swing that squeaked. To tell the truth, I was relieved, for that moment anyway. I was sure that our next trip to Grandma's would remind her of going to the park and heaven knows, we'd try again.

A little closer to our home now, there was a problem with crossing the street. We had worked on going to the corner, looking both ways, then crossing when it was safe. I also stressed the need to have an adult help her, but she seemed to forget that important bit of information from time to time…crossing by herself was a no-no and she found that out fairly quickly. I watched her as she crossed the street and made it safely to the neighbors (twice) and both times she had gone on her own. Silently, I was pleased with her success and I was thankful that no fast cars had zoomed by. I still felt she needed adult supervision, so I brought her back home and scolded her for her actions of venturing off by herself. I let her know the rules still stood, at least for the summer. With her head hung down, her eyes looking at her feet and her lower lip sticking out, she accepted her just punishment of being confined to our yard.

With every year and every time she tested her independence, I had to stop and think about what was actually happening. I knew she was intelligent, as she was always able to comprehend a variety of situations and knew what to do in case of an emergency. By the time she was eight or nine, I knew that she was able to go with me to the store and go down an aisle by herself, looking for that perfect treat or drink to buy. I knew that she could make her own lunch, albeit it was always the same, a couple of peanut butter crackers. But, there were times when her independent streak overpowered her understanding of a situation and mistakes were made. Well, I hoped that those mistakes were a learning curve for her and I believe that they were. Should she have tried to call the police because she heard a noise and it scared her because she thought she was home alone? Well, maybe not, because I was just in the other room. I guess I made the noise. After the officer made a return call to our house phone, just to make sure Lisa was safe, I explained to Lisa about the many situations where calling 911 was okay. So, the call she made was a slight mistake but after that Lisa knew what to do in an emergency. On a positive note, I think she benefited and learned from the experience.

When would be the right time to let her go, to be self-reliant, to grow up? My mind was willing, but my heart held fast. As Lisa continued to learn and grow, there were many times when I had to loosen those apron strings. But, I have been untying them very, very slowly.

Lisa As The Teacher

I have a sister who was a teacher in a grade school and one year when Lisa was in about 4th grade, my sister invited Lisa to go and spend a day in her classroom and share information about Down syndrome. This meant talking to Lisa more about her Down syndrome, which I had always done as she was growing up. But, I now thought I should remind Lisa of more details about the obvious characteristics like the simian line on her hand, the way the eyes slightly slanted and the fact that her ears are smaller and more low-set. The less obvious characteristics might include having that extra chromosome 21 or the fact that this involved having an intellectual disability.

I wanted Lisa to be able to know the answers so she could speak for herself, instead of me doing all the talking. On the drive to this small, rural town I would ask her questions just to see how she would handle the answers. Lisa did fine for the first few questions, then she kind of stopped talking. I guessed she was tired of the questions and maybe thought something like, "Gee, if mom is asking all these questions, maybe she needs to read up on Down syndrome a little more." So, I stopped asking questions on the road trip mainly because she stopped answering.

We arrived at the school after lunch and headed into the meet and greet. My sister had a projector set up and was ready to roll, but first she was going to give her students a little history and background about Lisa. My sister had prepared the slide show ahead of time by coming down to visit us, take pictures and asking lots of questions about Lisa and Down syndrome. She put the slide show production to music and she had useful information written on some of the slides. There were great pictures of Lisa as a baby, showing her at different stages of her development and all that she could do at a young age. This was good because it showed that Lisa was as typical as all the children in that classroom. I was thinking that this slide show would help break the ice and the students would embrace the opportunity to ask lots of questions of Lisa.

That didn't work out so well. The students asked questions but they were questions about which Lisa could not answer, like "How did this happen?" I told Lisa about her chromosome 21 but didn't explain when or why that would occur. And, now I wasn't sure if I could explain about cell division. I did explain about the different types of Down syndrome, starting with the type Lisa has, trisomy 21. There is also translocation and mosaic Down syndrome. People who have mosaic Down syndrome tend to have higher IQ scores and have less obvious features. The third type of Down syndrome is translocation, which affects about 4 percent of babies who are born with Down syndrome. It still is related with chromosome 21, but instead of the cell division showing three 21st chromosomes, the extra chromosome 21 is attached to another chromosome. The most mentioned chromosome attachment is to the 14 chromosome. Wow,

I must say, I think that was way too much chromosomal information.

At some point in time, the students asked Lisa questions about what she liked to do, what she liked to eat, what music she liked to listen to and other such topics that were better suited for Lisa to discuss. She did ok, even though her voice was quiet and she didn't always look at the person who asked her the question, nor did she look at anyone very often. She was sitting next to me in the school desk she was assigned to and she looked rather small in the oversized desk. Her feet dangled, so she sat cross-legged most of the time. And, she had to constantly pull at her dress or tights, depending on which was bothering her at any given time.

Another time during the Q and A period, my sister went over to Lisa to help her with her answers and my sister ended up getting Lisa out of the chair and had Lisa sit on her lap for part of the time we were there. I don't think anyone thought anything of this kind act, but I remember wondering if my sister would have done the same for any of her own students. But, hey, being Lisa's aunt gave her and Lisa some privileges, right?

So, this was Lisa's first time at giving answers to others in a formal setting, but it wasn't her last time in front of a crowd. Whenever Lisa went to a new school, she was part of the process of meeting the people who would be involved with her education and Lisa would answer questions when asked. When she was involved with a leadership program, she gave several speeches and I was told she did an exceptional job, speaking clearly and loudly and getting her point across effectively. When she was on local and state advocacy boards, she would give a speech when she wanted to run for an office and always told me later about the outcome. She was always very confident and composed, and a lot of times she would be elected to that position that she was running for on that board. So, she started off knowing about herself, being able to tell others and then show her capabilities and strengths. She became a spokesperson for herself and a voice for others.

The Innocent

Printed with permission of the author
Edna Massimilla

She thinks no evil - does no harm.
Her disposition is always calm.
So full of love and gladness too,
She only sees the good in you.
Anger, lust, they're not real.
Such normal impulses she doesn't feel.
She is innocent. This is true-
Of hate and fear and things we do.
Such perfect trust, so hard to find,
Exemplifies her peace of mind.
With eyes upturned and heart sincere,
Her thoughts may seem quite far from here.
A deeper knowledge, yet not expressed,
Perhaps she's wiser than the rest.
She's sweet and gentle; meek and mild,
She's our lovely Downs Syndrome child.

BARCUS

People-First Language Encouraged

It was in 1988 that I really became aware of using people-first language. A variety of establishments, like the Arc organization, different councils on developmental disabilities and advocacy groups made sure through different media channels to let the world know about the need for respect and consideration when talking about people with different skills and requirements. According to The Arc, "People with disabilities constitute our nation's largest minority group, which is simultaneously the most inclusive and the most diverse. Everyone is represented: of all genders, all ages, all religions, all socioeconomic levels and all ethnic backgrounds. The disability community is the only minority group that anyone can join at any time." [10]

People first language does not need to be used only in cases of describing a person with a disability, but can be used in other ways of identifying a condition instead of a person. Wikipedia used this example, to say "people who live on the street" rather than "homeless." [11] Of course, it takes more words and a longer amount of time to describe something when using the first description, but it avoids the embarrassment or humiliation that comes with the word homeless. Put the person before the disability. Also, don't say Lisa *is* Down's but instead say she *has* Down syndrome. Lisa is not her disability.

When using people first language, talk about someone with a disability and mention the disability second. An example to clarify this would be to talk about John, who has cerebral palsy, not talk about that cerebral palsied person, John. Another example is not to say that retarded person Sue, but say Sue, who has a developmental or intellectual disability.

Terms we use automatically in the past are no longer considered in good taste. A change I have always wanted to see is to delete the word retarded from the dictionary. I believe The Arc was leading the way when they changed the wording of the name of their national organization. From 1952-1973, they were known as the National Association for Retarded Children, (NARC) and then from 1974-1980, the name was the National Association for Retarded Citizens. In 1980, they changed the name to the Association for Retarded Citizens of the United States and finally, since 1991 they have been known as The Arc.

In 1990, I received a small brochure that was entitled "Guidelines for Reporting and Writing About People With Disabilities." There was a list of appropriate terminology that told the readers certain words are preferred words that reflect a positive attitude in portraying disabilities. For the term Down syndrome, the brochure explains that this is the proper term to describe a form of mental retardation caused by improper chromosomal division during fetal development. Mongol or mongoloid was unacceptable. I have never liked hearing or using the word retarded either, especially since I have a child with Down syndrome, a form of mental retardation. We do not deny the fact that she was born this way; we only prefer to say she is slow or developmentally delayed. Some terms just sound nicer than others and when using the positive words, this helps individuals with disabilities because, well, they are positive words.

The Arc started in 1950 by parents, because of a lack of programs and services available to help those with developmental disabilities and has become a national organization to help others in reaching their potential. The Arc's mission statement is as follows: The Arc promotes and protects the human rights of people with intellectual and developmental disabilities and actively supports their full inclusion and participation in the community throughout their lifetimes.

I know that Lisa, at age 11, questioned why she was the way she was and voiced her dislike about having Down syndrome. I tried my best to be open and honest about her disability, but in a positive way. She now knows the term Down syndrome, what it means, characteristics that are associated with the disorder and certain problems that may occur with Down syndrome.

Lisa has never been told she cannot do certain things, nor has she ever been called dumb, stupid or any other derogatory name by anyone in our family. Even though we didn't use the word retarded, she does know that it means slow and that is enough for her. She also refuses to be called handicapped, too. To be handicapped is not the same as having a disability. Handicap describes a situation not a person, such as a narrow doorway handicaps someone in a wheelchair. A person with a disability may consider him or her self handicapped, but this is self-imposed. I do not believe a disability and a handicap are the same. Maybe it's just a matter of semantics.

It's difficult for me to tell about Lisa's birth without bringing up the words retarded and mongoloid, because that is what my doctor told me when he first suspected that Lisa had Down syndrome. I did not know what the term Down syndrome meant, so even though the words were harsh, he had to find some way to explain the simple truth. I do not believe, or I guess I should hope that in 2016, doctors do not revert to the negative phrases that are no longer considered acceptable in today's language. Those negative words and phrases are not in my vocabulary and I hope that others agree with me that they should not be used. I have heard many adults advocating for themselves and who have openly share their feelings about having a disability. These people live and work in our communities and are shouting for a right to be treated like anyone else. They want others to look at what they can do; not just look at their disability. These people want to take the word retarded out of the english language. They want to be recognized as people who can learn, even though it may take them a little longer. It's that simple.

There are other groups who are also sensitive about the terminology used concerning their disability. It is appropriate to talk of someone who is visually impaired or blind, but some of these same people do not like to be considered partially sighted because it sounds like they have not yet fully admitted their disability. Saying the person is visually impaired is a more positive phrase. The Institute on Disability/UCED cites, "Some blind people consider themselves visual thinkers so they regard visually impaired and visually challenges as negative terms." [12]

It is acceptable for someone with a hearing loss to be considered hearing impaired, hard of hearing or deaf. Saying deaf mute is not appropriate. And using the words mute or dumb are not appropriate when describing someone with a speech disorder. Such a person would be without speech or they have a speech disorder. These terms may sound very similar and insignificant to most of us, but to those with a disability, the positive terms are more appropriate and accepting.

We have used many of these terms for years without thinking of their meaning or insinuations. I hope we have since become more aware of their harsh impacts because people with the specific disabilities are speaking up and voicing their dislike for labels. We can all make a difference by accepting people for who they are and by doing away with the outdated words.

Years ago, when I took a more active role in The Arc organization, I remember they had a coined phrase that went something like this: "The Arc is a local, state and national organization committed to securing for all people with mental retardation the opportunity to choose and realize their goals of where and how they learn, live, work and play." I encourage all of you to think about how you describe your neighbor or friend who has a disability. Let your words reflect a more positive attitude and use people-first language.

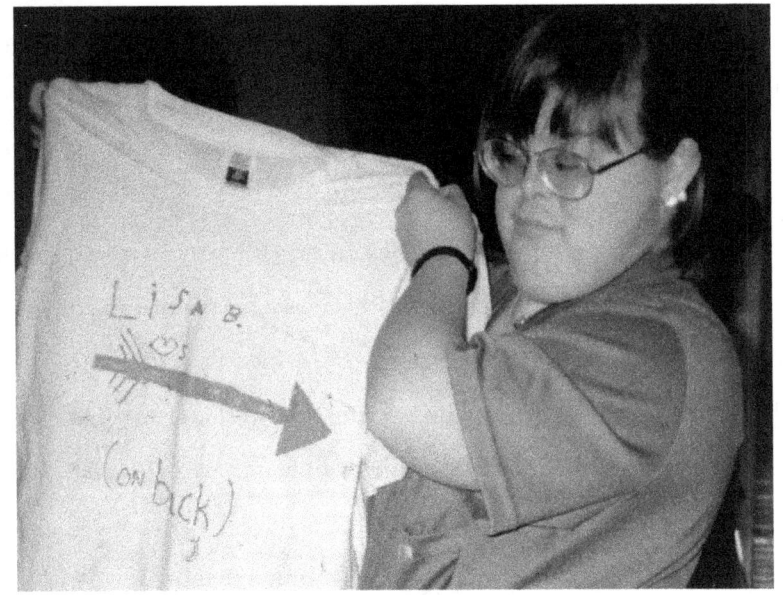

Preparing For Regular Education Classes

Lisa began her schooling at the young age of three months in a homebound program. She entered a toddler program at the age of three years old, attending several times a week for two hours at a time. At the age of five, she attended an Early Childhood program, being integrated with kindergarten children for some activities. At age six, she was in an all-day program with children of the same age for first grade. This was in a school across town and she rode a school van every day. Her classmates were from various parts of our town and surrounding towns that participated in the school program. The program was a Developmental Learning Program, (DLP) [13] where they taught more of the academics such as reading, writing and math. The other option for most children with a disability was the Independent Learning Program, (ILP) [14] that deals with skills of daily functions needed to live on their own. We felt Lisa had the potential to learn and we wanted to stress the academics. She attended the Developmental Learning Program through her fourth grade school year. She also attended eight weeks of summer school every year, which helped her to retain many of the more difficult concepts she had learned throughout the school year.

In 1989, we began to talk about the neighborhood school proposal with some of the school personnel. A school staff member, knowledgeable on the topic of the neighborhood school idea, went to visit at the neighborhood school and talked with staff about the model we were suggesting. This person also talked about Down syndrome, reassuring the school staff that these children are more like other children than not. We prepared the students who were in the classroom that Lisa would attend by having Lisa visit for three days in the spring, before her targeted arrival date. Lisa also brought along a poster of her likes and dislikes and listed some of her favorite things to do, to show the children how she is just like any student who would attend that school. Part of the preparation was with the help of a presentation called Circle of Friends. This program was a support system that helped students to be included in all areas, especially within the school system. Several educators were involved with the process, which would help make a smooth and efficient transition for Lisa to her new school setting. We had several meetings with staff on the concept of the program and finished discussing the details and everything was ready in time for Lisa to attend her neighborhood school in the fall of 1990.

Lisa went to a sitter before 8 a.m. and walked to school at the appropriate time. She was responsible for her own personal property and her actions. She had a routine that she learned within a short amount of time. She attended opening day with her classmates, a group of thirty-some fourth graders. We chose to have her repeat fourth grade for a second year, giving her a chance to mature a little longer. Her stature was slight and her level of learning was in the first to second grade range, so this action did not really draw any undue attention to her fitting in with her new classmates. She attended a resource room for several different studies, including reading, writing and math. She was in a science class with her classmates, as well as Social Studies. Lisa may have received help from others, but was encouraged to do as much as she could on her own. The teachers and other staff members adapted some of the course work for her. She adjusted well to her new school friends and was more outgoing in our neighborhood as well.

When she started at the neighborhood school full time, the friends she did not know before all these preparations now greeted her warmly. And, she would see her friends in school as well as after school. She became more mature in her actions and behaved appropriately. She gained a sense of self-worth and held herself in high esteem. I believe this was accomplished because of how she was treated by her classmates, as an equal peer and maybe even more significantly, as a friend.

We encouraged Lisa to participate in activities outside the school system, and she took a dance class once a week with other children. She also took swim lessons at our YMCA twice a week and attended an after-school day care for any student needing such a program. We also had her involved in Special Olympics roller-skating and swimming, and she also loved to bowl, but we usually did this only as a family activity. She became very self-confident and able to stand up for what she wanted. We were very pleased with all her progress.

The work to get her in the neighborhood school was well

worth the time and effort. We had lots of support from the schools and staff. The Circle of Friends plan was an intregal piece of Lisa's success in a regular educational, neighborhood school setting.

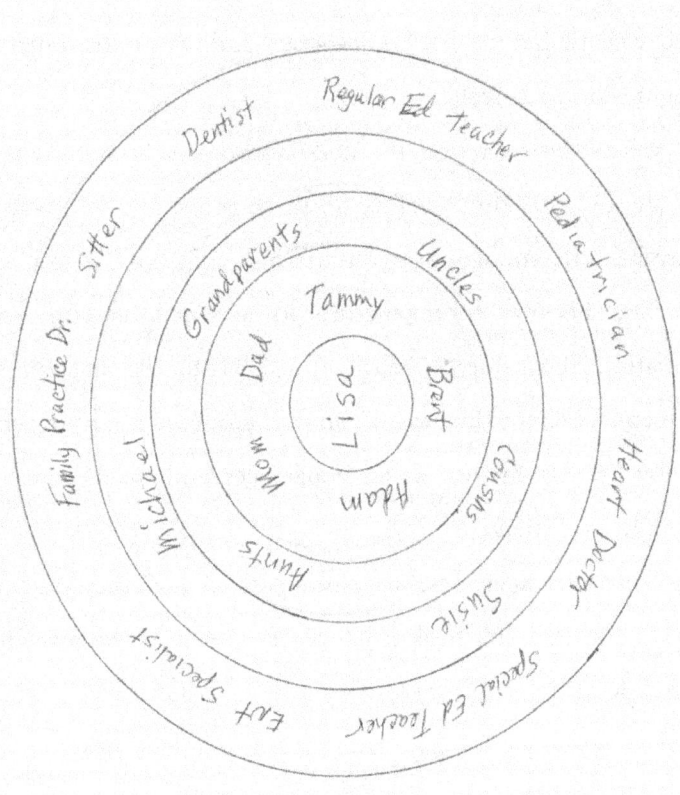

Circle Of Friends

I am sure that there are many wonderful accomplishments that have been met by children served in special education. For Lisa, her early years of school were in the special education programs and it was there that she received a solid basis for learning. Her skills developed at a slower rate than most students her age, but if compared to another with Down syndrome, she made terrific strides in learning. It was because of her capabilities and a need to develop more social skills that we, as parents, chose to have her attend our neighborhood school.

Special education was good for Lisa, but regular education classes were great! Lisa attended her neighborhood school, where her sister and brothers went, and it was a very positive experience. Lisa became much more social and learned appropriate behaviors from her peers. Well, sometimes she also learned inappropriate behavior, but I will tell you more about that topic later on. Furthermore, she became an outgoing, positive and self-assured young lady. Lisa was able to relate to others in her class and was welcomed as an equal. And best of all, she had friends in the neighborhood and in the school.

I truly believe this was the best action we could have taken on Lisa's behalf. She learned to act appropriately for her age, to be socially accepted and to be responsible for her actions. It took quite some effort to make this a positive and workable experience for all, but it was well worth it. Before the transfer to this neighborhood school, we had a parent of an older child with Down syndrome go to visit and to talk to the classmates, helping to reassure the students that a child with Down syndrome is no different than anyone else. Lisa also visited for several days, to become acquainted with the students and school layout.

When you have a person who plans to attend the neighborhood school after being in a self-contained classroom or similar setting, I would encourage some preparation by the family and teachers. Educators need to sit down with the family and discuss the student's strengths, weaknesses and needs. They can discover what to expect from that person, look for all possible trouble spots that may occur and formulate viable solutions. It is also handy to have a backup plan to survive any unforeseen incidences.

I don't think you can be ready for all that will occur; we definitely were not totally ready for the bumps in the road that we encountered. I think others need to be aware of the possibility that it may take some quick thinking to alleviate a problem or situation related to attending a new or different school setting. What we tried are just some ideas to get ready for a change like this and have it be a smooth transition. Remember each student is an individual and should be treated as such. There is no universal solution and no wrong solution if managed with the input of the student and family.

The teacher needs to be ready by having appropriate work material for the student and making sure the necessary auxiliary equipment is on hand. Getting help from other students is a big plus, allowing for normal integration among peers. My suggestion is the Circle of Friends program that encourages friendships in the classroom and school setting. We should all be a friend and have a friend. As Abraham Lincoln said, "The better part of one's life consists of friendships." And, Orson Wells said, "A friend is somebody who knows all about you, but likes you anyway." Where there is a circle of friends there is support for that person, and there can be interaction, communication and listening. There should also be genuine care and respect for that person. But, I digress; there will be more on the Circle of Friends topic later.

The teacher should treat the student like any other, giving appropriate punishment and rewards for their actions. Above all, teachers need to maintain a positive attitude. I believe full inclusion is the best school setting for all students, regardless of their limitations. To learn and grow with their peers is important for the acceptance in the community, now and for their future. These are a few of the actions we took when getting ready for Lisa to move to the neighborhood school. Some may work, others may not. But, keep trying; it's worth the effort when you see your child is with their peers, and is comfortable, well adjusted and happy.

One of the best proactive measures we used was an in-service for teachers, parents and the classmates of Lisa. Several teachers brought in the needed materials and we spent time learning about what the Circle of Friends approach was and how to implement it. I remember the first discussion was with the teachers. A specialist who had been using and had taught others about the Circle of Friends concept was going to give an overview, so Lisa's Dad and I attended to learn more about this timely program. It was a way to include Lisa in the classroom as well as making the classmates aware of Lisa's social history. It was about getting to know Lisa and encouraging others to be kind and respectful. It was about seeing Lisa as a person, just as we all are, and not about being different, though it also brought out that there were differences in Lisa's Circle of Friends.

We actually met with the specialist before the school meeting, where Lisa, her Dad and I were given homework to do before bringing this information to the school setting. We were instructed to draw a poster board sign showing who was in Lisa's circle. Are you ready? By the time I'm done explaining, it will feel like we are just going around in circles! Well, what this really amounted to was that we started by drawing Lisa's circle in the center. That would have just Lisa's name written in that circle. In the next circle that surrounded Lisa's center circle we listed Lisa's immediate family. This included her two brothers, a sister, and her Mom and Dad. After that, the next circle around the first two circles was a list of her other relatives. In circle number four, we listed her friends, but could only count those who Lisa played with on a regular basis. Not many names were in that circle, because she really didn't have many in her life at that time that she could really count as friends. After that, another circle was drawn around the first four and in this one we listed the professional people and other such people in Lisa's life. This final circle, which was drawn around all the other circles, was to include people in her life that did something for her, such as teachers, doctors, specialists, et cetera, that had some connection in her life. This was a very *long* list and a real eye opener for me. And, these people didn't necessarily volunteer to be with Lisa; most of them got paid to help her.

First up, doctors. Let's see; there was her family doctor, a pediatrician, her heart specialist and her otolaryngologist, (that's an ear, nose and throat specialist in English). Then there are the dentist, special education teacher, physical and occupational instructors, resource teachers, (yes, sometimes there was more than one resource teacher working with Lisa) and regular education teachers when she went to that classroom for part of her school day. I think we also mentioned the babysitter as well. I almost think there were even more than just these people that I have listed, but you get the idea. Lisa, as well as many other children who were in the special educational programs, had more people in the last circle of "paid friends" than in their friends and family circles combined.

After we completed the homework project, we brought it to the classroom where Lisa would be attending school later on that year. Any teacher who would be working with Lisa, the principal and the classmates were all in attendance. Lisa's Dad and I sat next to Lisa in those small desks, trying to get our knees to fit underneath, but ending up sitting a little crossways with our legs out in the aisle. Lisa, on the other hand, was sitting cross-legged in her seat with an occasional change of position, dangling her legs in front of her. She still couldn't touch the floor with her feet. I thought to myself, "This feat, excuse the pun, trying to touch the floor while sitting in a chair, will be a lifelong challenge."

Now, it was time for Lisa and the specialist to explain the big poster board full of circles we brought for show and tell. The specialist was wonderful, asking Lisa about her circles and waiting patiently while she reviewed each circle and whose names were written in and why. Lisa did wonderful, too. She was a little shy in the beginning, but began to find her voice and volume over time. The students and staff were wonderful, because they were attentive, showed interest and asked many specific questions. I was surprised by the children's reaction when the last circle, Lisa's paid people in her life, was explained. They got it. They saw that Lisa had too many paid specialists. The students were even asked to draw their own circles and again realized how few names showed up in that last circle. There was the difference in Lisa and her classmates' circles. There was the ah-ha moment when you could see that the children really got it. And that was the reason we went through this exercise. This was the best action we could have taken to get the point across. And, those classmates became her friends, because they wanted to be friends with her and not just because they had to be her friend. I must say, it was the turning point in the cycle of circles.

Years later, when Lisa was in high school, an organization nominated a high school teacher for a Teacher of the Year award. It was in part because this teacher was a big help in supporting Lisa. Here is part of the nomination letter that we wrote in support of that teacher:

"Moving to a new city and starting in another school can be scary and difficult for any student. Having an advocate in the school system helps the student through the adjustment period and this teacher has definitely been a positive support for Lisa at her new high school. The teacher has gone out of her way to make Lisa feel welcomed. Before school ever started, working after her regular school hours, on her own time, this teacher made several phone calls to the parents, as well as home visits. She spent time getting to know Lisa, her likes, dislikes and fears. The teacher took to time to discuss the high school, the classes available and what might be some appropriate choices based on Lisa's interests and comments. She also gave us a tour of the building prior to school starting, where we met several more teachers. This helped Lisa to be acclimated to the building layout, surroundings and classrooms.

Once school was in session, the teacher encouraged and assisted Lisa in using her assignment book for extra things, such as logging the names and phone numbers of her new friends. Lisa's assignment book was also used as a communication device between school and home, with the help and encouragement of this teacher. She took the time to correspond on pertinent school issues and activities, which has helped Lisa to be a part of after-school events.

The teacher has been known to still be at school after hours, making sure Lisa would get home safely. She also was considerate enough to call us when she could see a possible difficulty or uncomfortable situation for Lisa. For these times, this person always had an ingenious way of working things out to Lisa's benefit. She played a part in reaching a solution, never just the bearer of the impending dilemma.

The teacher has been very supportive in encouraging Lisa's personal and social growth. She has taken a positive and active interest in Lisa, caring about her well-being and future. I believe this teacher is a very conscientious and dedicated teacher; understanding, patient and kind. She has gone above and beyond what might be expected from a teacher. I believe her teaching must compliment her personal integrity, because Lisa comes home with such positive stories of her classroom experiences with this teacher. Consequently, Lisa loves school and learning. This teacher is a refreshing change from some of the educators in Lisa's past school situations. I believe this teacher would be a very appropriate choice for The Arc nomination of Teacher of the Year."

In my opinion, it is people like this who make the biggest impact in the lives of others. I am so glad we were able to have this person in Lisa's life. This teacher helped to build on Lisa's circle of friends and truly made a difference.

Inclusion, Integration, Transition

Circle of Friends worked well when Lisa transitioned from a school across town to a school in our neighborhood. That first year was like the honeymoon period, where the teacher did her best in treating Lisa like an equal and made her accountable for her actions. The teacher handled the changes in her *modus operandi*, allowing Lisa more time to get to her different classes, time spent in the restroom or time at the drinking fountain. Lisa had long ago figured out how to get out of class work or how to prolong trying not to do the work, so this was nothing new.

Of course there were glitches, but over all a great start with Lisa's integration to a regular education classroom setting. In a conference summary note that we received after the first 6 weeks of Lisa being in fourth grade at the neighborhood school, her classroom teachers made some notes about Lisa's progress. "Lisa loves science and tells us she shares that information at home. Lisa likes to sing so mom will work on the Christmas songs at home. The resource teacher says she is doing wonderful and working hard on her addition skills. Mom says Lisa is more outgoing and has gained new friends. In Physical Ed. Lisa has some fear of the ball, but a balloon ball seems appropriate. Dad plans to visit. The library reading, easy-to-read books, will be used during quiet time and to take home." Nice comments.

I came across a note that was written while Lisa was in fourth grade and it was from her best friend, whom I will not mention by name, but will share the note. On the front of the folded paper it had To: Lisa From: Your best friend. Then on the inside there was a drawing of two stick people, one labeled Lisa and the other labeled with the friend's name. The note reads as follows: "Lisa is nice and pretty, too. I like her a lot. She is my best friend." Below that is Lisa's response. Lisa starts off by writing the best friend's name saying, "She is nice and I like her a lot. She is my best friend. Thanks." Then on the back of the paper the best friend writes back saying, "Lisa, when I get done with my math I will take you to the library. Ok. Write back." Now I don't know which came first, the comment about taking Lisa to the library or the comment about saying Lisa is nice and pretty. My comment is, if this friend had just finished her math first, she would then have time to take Lisa to the library without writing the note. But, my other comment is, what a nice note. I also found a note from her fourth grade teacher, which says "Lisa, we are so very proud of you! The children and I are glad you won two blue ribbons. You are a very fast skater. I am so glad you got to go." (This was a Special Olympics event, where Lisa must have skated pretty fast!) As long as we are on teacher notes, here are a few more. A "Way to Go" award: for being in the right class at the right time. A "Super Bee-havior award for good listening." An "Egg"ceptional award for Lisa because she was a fantastic reader! A "Here's my Heart" award because she was a real hard worker today and another that says Lisa did great handwriting that day. So, fourth grade was very positive for Lisa.

In her second year there, now as a fifth grader, Lisa had a new teacher so there was a little bit of a learning curve for both the teacher and Lisa. The students did not have too many issues with Lisa, and Lisa seemed to thrive at being there. One of Lisa's best friends was in the same fifth grade, which I thought was a good setup. They both seemed to get along great and helped each other out in class.

With fifth grade, there were also few challenges. We know that this fifth grade teacher worked well with children because she taught one or two of Lisa's siblings in the past. We met ahead of time to review the IEP and related goals. We didn't have to go through the entire process with enlightening the students or the teacher because they were in on the first session before Lisa ever came to the neighborhood school. So, what went wrong? Nothing really, except that maybe Lisa was getting too comfortable in the new setting. The new setting was now old news and Lisa was just pushing her luck. The fifth grade teacher had to learn a few things about Lisa's tactics and Lisa had to learn that the teacher would not play the game. Lisa would not always respond in class nor would she always follow directions. Notes from the teacher asked for help in how to handle those situations. Lisa would try to get someone else to do her work or at least to help her with things that she had done on her own when in fourth grade. Again notes from the teacher asking for some guidance. Sometimes though, I didn't really know how to answer the teacher. One note said, "Lisa continues to need work on responding to people when spoken to. I've started trying to have her classmates give her the needed information as I thought maybe she doesn't want to listen to me. Do you have any other suggestions?" My first impulse was to write her back, noting that the "responding to people" situation was probably in her IEP goals, because from the time she was in preschool, she was always working on looking at the person talking and responding appropriately. There was only a little space on this teachers' note, so I simple wrote back "Perseverance!?!" Don't know if that helped her or not, but I do know that there were a couple more incidents before Lisa settled in to the fifth grade routine.

With both situations, Lisa was in cahoots with her best friend that she met in fourth grade. First, they were found in the classroom, eating chalk. Now, I don't know if there were other students around, whether the teacher was in the room at the time or if those two simply decided to skip lunch and sneak back up to the second floor classroom to eat chalk instead. We heard about this circumstance and I am sure we had a note from the teacher. I do not remember if there was any type of reprimand or consequence but I do know what happened next. Lisa and her best friend had to go to the restroom at the same time; imagine that. When they didn't return in a timely manner, someone was sent to see what was going on. Well, the two girls were busy trying to flush their shoes down the toilet! What for, you ask? No one knows. But, this was not acceptable and things had to change. And we didn't just mean with Lisa. We were also talking about the teacher. She had tried her best to teach Lisa and she was probably doing a great job. But, she was treating Lisa as if she had a disability. Oh, wait, she does. In Lisa's case, she needed to be treated like everyone else. And, I think the teacher was making adjustments for Lisa's actions and overlooking skirmishes that had been occurring. We talked to the teacher and got our message across. Treat her like any other student. If she does something wrong, there is a consequence. And, just that quickly, Lisa changed. She did act better, as noted by at least these two classroom awards. The first one I found in Lisa's stash of saved school mementos was a Good Listener award and as the award said "Lisa listened carefully today." The other award said, "Lisa went down to get a drink and came back right away."

Some of Lisa's report cards showed improvement in all subjects and comments about her were mainly positive. (Thank goodness.) And, on the report cards, the fifth grade teacher's remarks were as follows: "Lisa works well amongst her peers. We've established a workable routine and Lisa has shown a great improvement in using appropriate behavior as well as being responsible. Lisa has worked hard this quarter." The last progress report starts off well with "Had a great day until dismissal!" Then things turned sour. The teacher also wrote, "Lisa left before she received her progress report. I asked her to return to the room; she headed in the right direction when I was with her, but was found later on the steps. She stayed 10 minutes longer in detention." Darn. It was going so well up until then.

And now, here are some written report card comments about her physical ed. class. In 4th grade, the PE teacher wrote: For the horizontal ladder (arm and shoulder strength): If I hold Lisa's legs she will go across using her arms. In 5th grade, this same teacher wrote: With assistance she can do the horizontal ladder. In the Jog endurance work for 4th grade, the PE teacher wrote: If Lisa has a buddy with her she will jog but not for 5 minutes. For 5th grade, this same teacher wrote: Lisa walked and jogged with prompting. For the jump roping challenge in 4th grade, which involved endurance and coordination, the PE teacher wrote: Lisa holds the rope correctly, can swing it above her head, make a line with it on the floor and jump over it. For 5th grade, this same teacher wrote: Lisa swings the rope over and jumps when it is on the ground. Understands the mechanics of the crossover. For ball skills that encourage eye-hand coordination and agility, in both 4th and 5th grade, the PE teacher wrote: Lisa can dribble, bounce and catch a red rubber ball. Also, while Lisa was in 4th grade, the teacher added the comment: Lisa can't toss the ball in the air, clap 3 times and catch but she can do the rest of the routine.

So life in the neighborhood school moved on, and one day Lisa had to write a story in class. She named her book Fluffy and on the front it was noted that the book was written by and illustrated by Lisa. There was also a drawing of an orange cat with a large head and it looked like he had scratched the walls. Inside, Lisa dedicated the book to her resource teacher. Each page had a drawing of Fluffy and was depicted doing what that page had written on it. Each page was a different day of the week, and the story goes like this: "On Monday…Fluffy hopped into the fish tank. There were fish everywhere. On Tuesday…Fluffy walked in the mud. There was mud everywhere. On Wednesday…Fluffy ate all my canaries. She got fat. On Thursday…Fluffy broke the cup. There was glass everywhere. On Friday…Fluffy knocked over the pail, and there was water everywhere. On Saturday, Fluffy knocked over the plant. There was dirt everywhere. Tomorrow is Sunday…maybe Fluffy will play cards." This won a "Young Author" work award and she was able to attend a program where all the students were acknowledged for their accomplishments in writing a story. What a proud moment for everyone. And fifth grade finished without too many other incidents.

We were off and running in 6th grade, with the best surprise for Lisa being that her 6th grade teacher was the same teacher she had in 5th grade. That teacher actually asked to be Lisa's teacher in 6th grade, so 5th grade must not have taken too much of a toll on the teacher. Well, things were about to change, because Lisa's Dad had a change in his work situation. It would be a move to a different state, a different school and a different neighborhood.

We felt so settled where we were, with the kids' schools, neighborhood and activities. But, the change was a great opportunity, so we began to plan for the vision of what was to come. Change is difficult but sometimes necessary. William Pollard said, "To change is difficult. Not to change is fatal." I felt some anxiety with the whole idea of moving, especially to uproot the children and more specifically for Lisa, for she would have to move from a school that had welcomed her, worked with her and accepted her despite some misgivings on their part. That was going to be a big change for us, but this new change could be an adventure, to watch Lisa grow even more. Her siblings were a little more hesitant but in the end the decision was made. We would be moving.

In order to make the transition smooth for Lisa, we began the process by looking at the town we would move to and check out the school system first. We made a couple visits to this town, to talk to the Special Ed. Director and talk about what school would be the best placement for Lisa. We did this first, so we would know what neighborhood to look at when buying a house. The director was very cordial and helpful. He gave us some input as to which schools might be more appropriate for Lisa. She would be transferring after the Christmas break, so there was plenty of time to prepare the new staff and students to know a little bit about Lisa. We asked the director for some specific changes to the way their school district taught children with developmental disabilities. We knew we wanted Lisa in a regular ed. classroom with resource help. We asked for other minor things but mainly we wanted her to be in a classroom setting that would be offered to any child who came into that school district. The director was very upfront with his comment, "Well, we have never done that before" and I immediately thought "Oh, no. We won't be getting the placement and help we want for Lisa," but he finished his sentence by saying, "but we will try it." Wow, I thought to myself, 'It does pay to be an advocate.' To ask for something in the hopes that it could be possible; we were very pleased with that visit. (About three years later, we would be moving on to another state and town.) Before that happened, we were at a state convention for the Arc and that same Special Ed. director was there to accept an award, one that we had nominated with the school district in mind for all the work they had done to appropriately include Lisa. He approached us later and said thank you. He went on to say that if we hadn't moved to that town and asked for the things we did, the district would not be there at the convention accepting an award, because they probably would not have had a need to change. So, change is difficult, but good.

When we first prepared for the big move from our home state to this new state and to a new school, we looked again at using the Circle of Friends program, since we had such good success the first time. Because of the distance between the old and new schools, (some five and a half hours drive) we had to think outside of the box to get our ideas and views across. We first had Lisa make a smaller version of her circles and we sent it off to the classroom where she was already registered to go to when the second semester would start. After that, Lisa's classmates and teachers made a video that was sent to the new classmates so they could learn more about Lisa. It showed Lisa in her regular classroom, working at her desk, at the blackboard, in the gym eating lunch, going out to play, walking the halls to her resource room, music class and P.E. They depicted a typical day for a typical student. What happened next was really neat. The soon-to-be classmates sent back a video of their own. They showed Lisa her soon-to-be new classroom and the students in the video would wave, say hi, comment on something in the classroom and shared little tidbits that would be useful when she attended there. They used the video to walk down hallways, to other classrooms and outside, so that Lisa might become somewhat familiar with the layout ahead of time. Along with the video, the teacher wrote on a handmade, construction paper Christmas stocking, "Because we knew so much about you, your new friends wanted to do something to help you get to know them and your new school. This is an unedited video of a tour of our school and the teachers who help us. They were excited about making it. We hope you enjoy it! P.S. This was our first attempt at using the camera. Shortly after you arrive we will begin working on our highlight film." Lisa received many handwritten letters that were glued on a handmade, construction paper Christmas stocking. Those children shared some neat things, like "Hi, Lisa. My name is Joshua and I like the Kansas City Chiefs. My favorite TV show is 'Hanging with Mr. Cooper.' I am glad you are coming!" Another wrote, "Dear Lisa, That's my name too. I'm in dance class just like you and I'm looking forward to meeting you. Lisa" Tiffany wrote saying, "I am really excited for you to come. I look a little different now because I got a perm. I can't wait to sit by you! I can't wait to see you." The class teacher wrote, "I hope you enjoy the video. Our class enjoyed making it for you! Hugs, Mrs. B."

One of the saddest things that came about was Lisa leaving her friends in the neighborhood, those friends and classmates at the school and other acquaintances who lived near our house. Lisa received one note that was written in crayon, and decorated with a large, full-branched Christmas tree. It had bulbs in a variety of colors and other decorations hanging from those green branches and there were boxes of many shapes and sizes tied up with bows. The note said, "Lisa, I will miss you. You are my friend. I had fun playing with you, riding bikes. I will miss your brother, too. Farewell to you, Lisa. I hope you have a good time in your new town. Your friend."

The school Lisa was leaving and the one she was headed to did *so* much work and guess what, it helped with the transition. Our old house sold quickly, we found a new house in that new town that suited our needs and the school district turned out to be really great. The teachers were very supportive of our requests, of course I'm sure with some reservations. But, they tried, and that's what matters most. Lisa was only in this 6th grade class in this new school for half a year, since we moved between Christmas and New Year's, but it was a great success.

    Lisa adjusted to the new school rules, made some new friends and seemed content in where we were. She had a bedroom of her own, while her brothers shared a larger bedroom that just looked like it was meant for boys. Lisa was able to pick out a new bedspread and curtains, and was lucky enough to move up from a twin bed to a double size bed. Her bedroom was large enough to have that size bed in it, and it was also considered the "spare bedroom" when we had out of town guests stay over. Well, maybe Lisa wasn't lucky enough, because when guests came she was booted out of her room and she had to sleep on an air mattress, twin size, in the lower level of the house. Hum, she never really complained about that. Over the almost four years that we lived there, Lisa made several signs that she put on her bedroom door to decorate it, or maybe she really meant what the signs said. I came across several of theses signs in a storage box we used to save some of Lisa's memorabilia. The first one was definitely written by her, in pink magic marker. The words 'Lisa's room' was printed in very large letters on a white piece of printer paper, from my printer, I'm sure. Underneath that, with smaller pink magic marker letters it says, "Come in boys." Yup, she was a typical girl, always watching out for those cute boys to come around. The next sign was on a deep red piece of construction paper and the letters seem to be printed by someone other than Lisa. They are nice and evenly space, same height and width, almost a stenciled-looking shape and some of the letters are colored in with black magic marker. It says, 'Do not enter. My room.' There is a skull and cross bones hand-drawn picture with the eyes and nose blackened in. My handwriting was in the lower left corner, in a nice little print with a black fine point marker that says, 'Nice try!' I think she got the idea very quickly. I was still the mom, and even though she was now a teenager wanting her privacy, I was going to enter the room if need be. Of course, I respected her privacy and always knocked first. We had an understanding and it worked for us.

For Lisa's 6th grade graduation there was cake, ice cream, awards and an autograph book for teachers and students to sign. I won't rewrite all those accolades, but let's just say most of them were very nicely written greetings, compliments and praises for the friendships of many classmates throughout the year. The autograph book had a printed list of questions and the specific, individualized answers each student gave. Here are Lisa's answers. Favorite school lunch: Pizza. Worst school lunch: Macaroni. Favorite subject: Science. Worst subject: Spelling. Future Goals or Plans: Keep your hands and feet to yourself. Hum, I think she might have misunderstood that question or that answer got written on the wrong line of the questionnaire. Oh, well. Maybe it *was* a goal of hers.

A Vacation For The Family

When the kids were little, we didn't do many family vacations, mainly because of finances and past family tradition. I didn't grow up taking a yearly trip with the family and I think my husband only had a few trips with his family during his growing up years. So, when we talked about trips as a family, we had to think outside of the box. Short trips included visiting the big city and going to the zoo. Those were probably just day trips, so we left early in the morning, driving around two hours to reach our destination. We had a green, 12 passenger van and each child had their own bench seat. Lisa sat in her car seat right behind her Dad, who was in the driver's seat. I was in the front passenger seat, so I could check on Lisa by simply turning to my left and seeing her clearly and quickly. Lisa's bench seat was a short seat, only spanning about two-thirds of the way across the van. It allowed other passengers who were getting into the van to access the next bench seat behind the shorter seat that was Lisa's.

The next two seats, which were longer, were occupied by her brothers; one brother per seat. These seats came in handy because the boys could stretch out, lying down and have a nap when we drove any long distance. They always had their seat belts on but could lie down just the same since the belts were not shoulder straps, just the waist seat belts. The last seat, back near the rear door, was reserved for Lisa's older sister, who spent a lot of time reading. She kept busy and seemed to enjoy not having to share a seat with her younger siblings. We almost always packed a lunch, which consisted of peanut butter (and sometimes jelly) sandwiches, chips and juice drinks or maybe canned soda products. If there was dessert, it was probably those individually wrapped baked pie, chocolate cake or other such lunch items I bought at the day-old bread store. I thought they were a treat for the kids and it was easier than baking dessert to take along. (I don't think I'd pack a picnic lunch like that today. Hopefully, over the years I've learned something about good, healthy nutrition.)

On the drive, Lisa usually slept. Sooner or later we arrived, and typically it was a little later than we planned due to unscheduled potty breaks or an emergency diaper change for Lisa when she was younger. We made it safely to our destination, got out our hats or ball caps to shade our heads from the blazing sun and unfolded the small, portable red umbrella stroller. Then off we'd go, to look at the animals at the zoo, take some time at the petting area and riding the train and tram when we needed a walk break. Lisa rode in the stroller most of the time, but we let her venture along the walk ways when the areas had some flat places. I think all the kids loved the zoo and the picnic lunch when they started getting hungry. Lisa never complained much, unless she was sick or not feeling well, usually due to ear aches and ear infections. Later on, once or twice we had trips that took us to the big metropolis of Kansas City, to an amusement park, where the main attraction was all the rides, big and small. Lisa could spend hours on the kiddie roller coaster and other rides for younger and smaller children. At first, I wondered if they would even let her ride these kiddie rides, due to possible height recommendations listed or just for the fact that she had Down syndrome. Neither seemed to be an issue, until she got older. Then, the height requirements were a bummer. She was limited to a few adult rides, so we kept taking her back to the younger kids attractions. She could still fit in the small roller coaster cars and go by herself. If we let her, she could spend hours riding the three-minute attraction, get off, run around to the entrance, get on and ride again, again and again. All I had to do was sit and watch, while my husband was in charge of the other three children, who were busy running in all directions, wanting to go on the larger and faster roller coasters.

There was another trip to Kansas City that was rather unique in how it came about. As I said before, we had moved to another state in December, when Lisa was half way through her sixth grade school year. In the spring of that school year, Lisa received an invitation from her old sixth grade class to meet at the Kansas City amusement park. Since we only lived about two hours from Kansas City, we said yes to Lisa meeting up with her previous classmates for the day. She had a great time seeing everyone and they, too seemed pleased to see Lisa. I'm not sure she was able to ride all the same rides as the others, but she was able to be with them, play, laugh and run around with a great group of kids. Even the rain shower didn't dampen anyone's spirits.

Besides the zoo trips and the couple of times we went to Kansas City, we also took a couple trips to South Dakota. Once or twice we went to visit relatives, but there was another time when we went there to do some sight seeing. It was fun to take in the sights and activities that we didn't have in Nebraska. A fun place was to go to Mount Rushmore, where we walked around and looked at the monument. Lisa wanted a souvenir so she bought a postcard of the four presidents. We went to Dinosaur Park, where the kids could climb on the bright green concrete dinosaurs. Lisa wanted a souvenir of a dinosaur, so we got her some dinosaur eggs that could be hatched later on. Inside was a plastic dinosaur that she could play with, and she was thrilled with that. We also went to the Reptile Gardens, where we walked around looking at and touching all the different reptiles housed there, had some fun with the silly mirrors that made you look short and fat and enjoyed sitting on the large turtles. (They don't allow that anymore, but back then that was a real treat for the kids.) Lisa wanted a souvenir of a snake, so she purchased a rubber snake that got thrown around between all the kids, each trying to scare the other at the most unexpected time. By now, those souvenirs are long broken, misplaced or gone, but we still have the photos and the memories of fun times when the kids were growing up.

We didn't take many trips while the kids were younger but once they were on their own and more so after they were married, we invariably took some trips together. Lisa was always included, unless she had to work, which was most weekends. But, on special trips we made sure that she, too could be a part of the fun trips. The Cayman Islands was a destination wedding of one of Lisa's brothers, so we ALL definitely wanted to go there. By this time, there were three grandchildren added to the mix, which made the trip even more fun. Lisa wanted a souvenir, but she had sensibly graduated to wanting a t-shirt or refrigerator magnets. The t-shirt was usually what she chose to buy. A trip to DC started off as a golf trip for Lisa's brothers and Dad, and then they needed a fourth golfer, Lisa's sister. This then turned into the entire family going and spending a long weekend together. As usual, Lisa wanted a souvenir and she again picked out a t-shirt. No surprise there. Lisa has t-shirts from every trip she has taken as an adult and yet she wants more t-shirts. It seems to be on her list whenever anyone asks what she wants for her birthday or Christmas. What fond memories of those early trips, where we tried to figure out where we could take the kids, be it for a day trip to the zoo or a weekend trip to Kansas City. And, we continue to be making many more memories with the wonderful family trips, which usually include spouses and grandkids. And with each trip she goes on, Lisa seems to always want a souvenir; a t-shirt.

School Notes, Reports And Quarterly Remarks

I came across a mountain of saved papers from Lisa's middle school days, which at that time was specified as grades seventh and eight grade in that town. It was a new transition for her and for the teachers, since this was not the town or school district where our other children went and the teachers knew very little about Lisa. The middle school teachers received information from the teachers in 6th grade, and those teachers didn't know Lisa very well either because of the short amount of time Lisa had in that grade school at this new town. I guess four and a half months just wasn't enough time to really know Lisa like her prior grade school teachers did. And getting her class selections for seventh grade was a struggle. We wanted her in a regular education classroom, but teachers were wary of having her in their classroom even though Lisa had been in a regular classroom since the fourth grade. We wanted her to do as much of the same studies that the other students were in, be it in Art, Music, PE or other such classes. After a few meetings, we agreed on a workable solution for all involved. School started and I held my breath. It was interesting to see over the next two years how the comments on the progress reports changed. In the beginning, there were notations about her adjusting and learning the routine. The teachers would also comment about her having a good attitude or that she was "doing well." I have taken the liberty of categorizing the different subjects Lisa took and have listed some of the comments by teachers over a two-year period. Hope this doesn't bore you too much.

LD (Learning Disability) Math: Shows no initiative, does not request extra help. (Of course she wouldn't; math has never been her strong suit and if she asked for help or tried to do the math work, the teachers would be on to her that she *could* do the math, and then she would be stuck *doing* the math. So that comment didn't surprise me.) Note to readers, that was my comment. Comments later on included: "Does well on assignments" and "does better one on one but tries to work on her own." The teacher also suggested that Lisa could use a "checker" for math problems. I don't think they meant like the round, black or red piece used in the game of Checkers, but probably meant for her to follow-up or check her work using the math problem answers page in the back of the book to see if her answers were correct, and in this manner she would have learned the process of how someone got to that answer she was checking. Well, let's just say that's what the teacher meant. But, the best comment was during her 8th grade year, when they wrote: "Working on two digit multiplication, with and without carrying; good so far." What? Multiplication? How is that possible that she could do that? Especially with her aversion of math in general. Way to go, Math teacher. You broke through Lisa's hidden barrier and helped her in doing math without a struggle. Or at least, I never got any news that there was trouble. Maybe middle school teachers just learn to handle those types of situations.

In English, her first quarter progress report showed her grade as a big, fat, red F and the comment was she was below the class average by a lot. Well, I could have told them that, too. Other comments in the beginning quarter of school were: "Does not request help" and "Does not show initiative." But, by the end of 8th grade, some of the comments were: "Assignments handed in and they are very good." "Doing well in class and has positive attitude." This kind teacher also wrote that Lisa does participate in class and has good interaction with other classmates. The best comment: "Lisa is using the phonebook, is able to alphabetize and has story comprehension." Lisa had to write a story for a class assignment and then turned in her essay, entitled The Pet. It goes like this: "I could have a pet cougar. He would be kind of fast and he is not like a cat or a dog. I do have pet dog named Husker and he is mostly grayish black. He likes to sleep and eat, and he can jump up and down, dance and speak. He sleeps with his paws in the air. He likes it when I pet him while I watch TV. He sticks his nose under the covers." Lisa was also very artistic and drew a picture of Husker, the Schnauzer/Poodle mix with his long, floppy ears and tail wagging. The teacher put a big, multi-colored WOW sticker on the report and wrote that it was a great picture of the dog and that she liked the story.

Physical education class was not adaptive so Lisa was in a regular setting, trying to do all the things that other seventh and eighth graders were doing for PE. Beginning comments included things like "Does not work individually" and "Is not cooperative." By the end of eighth grade, the comments were more positive, like "Doing well" and "Acceptable/average" class work. But, the best comment was that Lisa was learning different dances in the dance unit and kept up with the other students. The teacher did mention that Lisa does go into passive resistance when she becomes uncomfortable. My comment: Don't we all? I did enjoy one last comment the teacher shared, which was that Lisa had come some distance in her overall development, socially and mentally. Wow, this regular education classroom setup really turned out to be a positive experience for Lisa. She had grown in leaps and bounds.

Lisa did have issues about being on time to class in the beginning, but I am sure that she was just trying to see how much she could get away with at this new setting and new teachers. That's normal, I think. She also only had or I should say *has* one speed and that's slow. So, if classrooms were spaced out too far, she would almost invariably be late unless there was a student to accompany her, urging her to hurry up before she is counted tardy. When she went to high school in this town, one of the ninth grade LD teachers had even written up a two page layout of things Lisa needed to work on, which included directives like "Lisa will be on time to each class with 100% accuracy as recorded by staff, Lisa will complete tasks/assignments on time for each class as recorded by staff and Lisa will learn a minimum of 10 new vocabulary terms for each regular education class using them appropriately in written and oral modes of communication as recorded by staff." There was a place on the sheets to mark if a goal was met, how many times and there was also a number grade assigned. I am sure they were trying to encourage some growth in Lisa's learning and keeping track of her success was beneficial. I personally think that was a great idea. These teachers who were hesitant to have Lisa in regular education classes sure stepped up and did it right. And for that, I am truly grateful. She was also absent more often than I would have wanted, but she still got ear infections and upper chest colds quite a bit. I don't believe that was ever an issue that we worried about too much, mainly because I don't remember getting any calls or notes saying Lisa was in jeopardy of being considered truant or needing to repeat a class.

Early comments from the teacher in the Keyboarding class Lisa took in ninth grade included things like "Lisa uses two hands when I am watching, otherwise she uses one finger to type" or "She has a tendency to quit before the hour is up" and "She has begun to smile and respond in class." But, the best comment was actually typed on an official form with the heading "In school suspension report." (ISS) It was very official looking and it was the one and only time we received anything from this teacher on a typed form letter. The cause for ISS had lots of checklist options to choose from such as fighting, profanity and vandalism, which I knew that Lisa would never do. Or so I thought. The space at the very bottom of all the options was marked with a BIG, black X and it had Other (to enter an explanation) next to that X if the above options were not an appropriate choice. The comment written in said: "Lisa took the track ball out of a computer mouse and threw it across the room. We have not been able to find the ball and Lisa will be charged for any needed repair to the mouse."

Now, I don't remember ever getting a bill for any repairs and

I don't remember Lisa being too overly concerned about the whole incident. She did not explain her actions, except to say "I just wanted to do it." At the end of the school year, I do remember finding a small, round ball in her bedroom when we were packing to move to another town. At the time, I couldn't figure out what it was, until I went to do some work on our home computer. That was an "ah-ha" moment for me and all I could do was remember the note and laugh. It was the ball to the school's computer mouse!

Finishing up the ninth grade high school year was somewhat familiar, because we had known for a while that Lisa would not be attending that high school for tenth grade. We were making another move, to another state. I know kids are resilient and can handle changes, but I just thought where we had been for the last three and a half years was working wonderfully in regards to Lisa, her having friends and her being able to attend regular education classes in a typical setting. But, the challenge then became a look ahead at what was to come, where we would live and what school would be chosen to carry on with what we had started in this town we were leaving. I hoped that the next school would be as accommodating. We did not know what was ahead, and we were unknowingly naïve and trusting enough that the same adaptions would be considered in this new school environment that we were heading to, but it didn't quite work out that way.

My Baby Sister-A Personal Essay

(Lisa's older brother, Brent, wrote the following sometime between 1995 and 1998. He thought he had written it for a college entrance requirement.)

On May 20, 1980 my baby sister was brought into this world with all the magic and luster any birth is given, but the gift of life came with an elucidating surprise. Upon arrival, we were greeted with the news that we had a brand new baby sister and that she had Down syndrome.

At the age of three and a half, I was unable to grasp the magnitude of this event, but I understood the trauma it inflicted on my parents. I was told that Down syndrome meant that she was born with an extra 21st chromosome. It was mentioned that she might have to be placed in an institution because at this time many people still held the belief that the mentally handicapped were not capable of pursuing a 'normal' life. This was very difficult for me to understand at that time. It was my belief, at my naïve age, that an extra 21st chromosome would make her super-intelligent. This perception is one that I still hold today.

The baby's birth raised many internal conflicts with my parents and with our family's beliefs and convictions, the most immediate being the question of institutionalization. Although acceptable to society, was institutionalization a practice acceptable with our family's morals and values? Was it righteous to slight the responsibility and the gift that God had granted? Financially, were we able to support this blessing? The conclusion to this dilemma was that we had been given this opportunity for a purpose and it was our responsibility to make the best out of what God had given us. This decision was the cross roads of life's path which led to the epiphany of all who come in contact with Lisa.

Three months after she returned home from the hospital, Lisa started home schooling. Other than Lisa being in school almost her entire life, she received no special treatment from my parents and especially from her siblings. My parents had to deal with three children all within three years of age, and the older sibling who was seven and a half. We had to fight for the attention of our parents just like a normal family. My parents quenched this problem by involving us all in the duty of educating Lisa and inevitably ourselves.

When Lisa started her schooling, she was unable to sit up on her own. My father engaged our assistance in building a platform that allowed her to sit up at an angle. From this point on we worked as a team to accelerate her progression, which led to our own advancement. Teaching Lisa the things that we took for granted also taught us to respect those less fortunate, but ultimately her example taught us that we could overcome any adversity set in our path through dedication and perseverance.

As children, my little sister and I would engage in conversation on excursions to the local gasoline station, reminding me that I was becoming overwhelmed by life's details and I had forgotten the overall beauty life holds. As we walked, she asked things like, "Why did that cat eat the mouse? Why is that person honking their horn? Why are the leaves different colors?" As she grew, so did her questions. At school one day, she had a conflict with her classmates in which they called her retarded; I asked her what she said to those kids. She had replied that she wasn't retarded, "It just takes me longer than other kids to learn things...Brent, why do people make fun of me?" It was with that comment that I began to think of what normal really meant. It was my first impulse to tell her she wasn't normal, but after much contemplation I realized this was far from the truth.

Everyone is unique in his or her own right; therefore, the definition of normal is an absolute. She sees no difference in her life compared to those around her. She struggles to overcome the obstacles which life presents her; she fights to change the stereotypical perception of society and still holds a love for the uncompassionate world around her, purely for the joy of life.

I quickly realized that this contingency we faced at her birth wasn't a negative obstacle but a stepping-stone, which brought our lives to a new appreciation. Who would have thought in 1980, under the question of institutionalization, that Lisa would be graduating high school next year, ready to take her place, contributing to the development of the world? Who would have thought that she would hold a part time job? Who would have thought that this child would be able to walk and live independent from others care? Lisa's influence over my life has been astronomical. As I watched her grow,

BARCUS

I was inspired by her dedication to achieve that which was thought impossible. Her undying devotion to success fueled by her love of life led me to develop a similar stance in my endeavors.

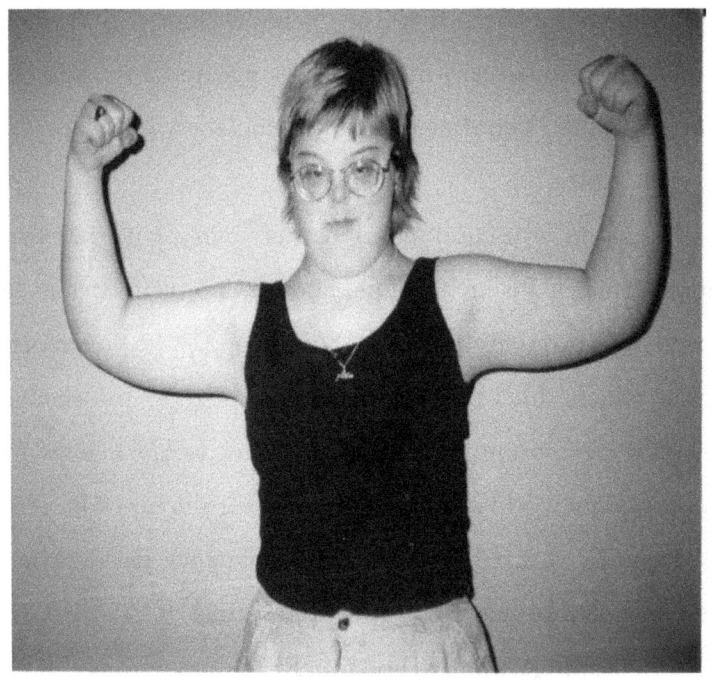

Thoughts On Inclusion

I am sure that in the early 1980s, special education services were on the cusp of what has since become the norm for students who need some extra help. Until Lisa came along, I knew nothing about special education services or the fears I had that went along with this somewhat uncharted territory. I also realize that some parents who will read the following may wonder about my viewpoint, since so much has changed from the 1980s to the present time in the field of special education. It just makes me smile to know that so many good changes have come about, not because of me, but because all those who have cared about the future of the school children who have a disability. What I wrote back in the early 1980s was as follows:

"In the early 1980s, there were changes in the school system that involved having children with developmental disabilities attend regular school programs, and at best, in their neighborhood school. The word inclusion was used and when stated, meant that the child who had a disability would attend the school that they would normally attend if they did not have a disability. Some of these changes came about because of the work of many educators who believed this was a step in the right direction and because of Public Law 94-142. This is the Education For All Handicapped Children

Act of 1975 and when it was passed it guaranteed that each child who had a disability would be allowed a free appropriate public education. According to the U.S. Department of Education, this law has four purposes:

Four Purposes of P.L. 94-142

1 "to assure that all children with disabilities have available to them ... a free appropriate public education which emphasizes special education and related services designed to meet their unique needs

2 to assure that the rights of children with disabilities and their parents ... are protected

3 to assist States and localities to provide for the education of all children with disabilities

4 to assess and assure the effectiveness of efforts to educate all children with disabilities"

Source: *Education for All Handicapped Children Act*, 1975

The U.S. Department of Education site also says 'P.L. 94-142 was a response to congressional concern for two groups of children. The law supported more than 1 million children with disabilities who had been excluded entirely from the education system. The law also supported children with disabilities who had had only limited access to the education system and were therefore denied an appropriate education. This latter group comprised more than half of all children with disabilities who were living in the United States in the early 1970s. These issues of improved access became guiding principles for further advances in educating children with disabilities over the last quarter of the 20th century.

Through such sustained federal leadership, the United States today is the world leader in early intervention and preschool programs for infants, toddlers, and preschool children with disabilities.' " [15]

Lisa was one individual who benefited from these changes. Lisa has attended some type of special educational program since the age of three months. Then, in fourth grade she had a major change in her school placement. She attended our "neighborhood" school, the same school where her brothers and sister were educated. In all her years of school, this was not a suggested option for her until we heard about it and looked into this as a possible change in her educational setting. Sadly enough, before 1975 a lot of children with a developmental disability were not in a normal school setting. They were either instructed at home, in institutions or in special self-contained classrooms. With the passing of Public law 94-142, we were finally allowing these children a chance to function as close to normal as possible. Lisa attended a regular fourth grade classroom with some resource help. Part of her day was designed for her to have some specialized help in reading, math and literature. She would leave the classroom during those time periods but did so on her own, and without disturbing the rest of the class. She attended PE, music, art and science with the rest of the class. She adjusted well and seemed to love the changes at the new setting, her neighborhood school

Inclusion brought numerous positive results, for Lisa as well as for others who came to know her. And hopefully, Lisa's attendance in her new school helped alleviate some people's thoughts of viewing her as different. It is my belief that by having Lisa included in regular education classes and in the world around us, the children and all of society can be more accepting of her and can hopefully relate to her as a person. In the neighborhood school, Lisa had typical children to model and learn from. Those same typical children also benefited by helping Lisa in learning, and hopefully they grew up to accept and enjoy Lisa as a friend.

My hope for Lisa was that she would increase her social skills, to make friends that she could be with after school hours and to be accepted without judgment from others. This early integration was a positive influence for all involved."

The terms integration and inclusion probably had some opposition initially. The demands that are placed on the teachers and other children may have also seemed great. There might have been concerns that the child with the disability may need more attention from the teacher compared to the other children in the classroom. The teachers may have wondered if they would be able to handle the additional challenges of a child with a disability. And would the teacher accept this additional role that is being placed on them? I am sure there were concerns on this topic that were voiced by teachers. I believe they were resolved when we, as Lisa's parents, along with the teachers she would have, worked together to get Lisa, the classmates, the teachers and the school ready for Lisa's new school setting.

Lisa adjusted well to her new surroundings. I believe transition was made easier because of in-house preparations before she started in her new school. In-services on Down syndrome were presented to both students and staff. Lisa also made a three-day visit in the spring before her targeted admission date in the fall. She was more comfortable with the proposed concept after her exciting visit and I'm sure the teachers appreciated some hands on experience with Lisa. In order for inclusion techniques to be successful, teachers, children and parents must have an understanding of the different disabilities, know that problems may occur and maintain a positive attitude for the individual educational plan (IEP) of each student.

We reviewed Lisa's IEP and made corrections or changes before she went to her neighborhood school. We made sure to have definite, attainable goals for Lisa. We also looked at her abilities and on-going success when deciding what could be done in the neighborhood school setting. Sometimes, the regular education teachers may need additional training in some cases to benefit the child who was being transitioned to their neighborhood school. I believe we tried a couple different ways to help the teachers know more about Lisa, her abilities and our hopes for her schooling. I do know that there was at least one in-service where we went to talk about Lisa and answer any questions the teachers and school staff might have about her. There was also a resource teacher in the building who helped provide for the specific services that Lisa needed in her academics. This resource teacher was also involved in educating other teachers and staff, helping with modifying lessons and giving direction or encouragement to the regular education classroom teachers.

Since Lisa's first move from a self-contained, special education classroom to the neighborhood school with her peers, there have been many people who helped with the transition and inclusion issues. In 2017, there are now many, many opportunities, organizations and connections to help and allow others to be fully included, not just in schools but also in their local communities and the work place, and basically in society itself. There are people with physical disabilities, learning disabilities, mobility impairments, health deficiencies, mental health issues and other situations where inclusion issues could arise. I am sure that with the help from people who care about others and with the tools and guidance from such laws like Public Law 94-142, we can be encouraged by the fact that others are also being helped to reach their full potential.

A Mother's Love

What are some of the activities that happen in February? According to the calendar, there are many events or occasions that mark the month of February. There is Mardi Gras, Ground Hog Day, President's Day and in the United States, mid-February is usually when some grade schools celebrate their 100th day of the school year. Of course, one of the most recognized and probably most celebrated would be Valentine's Day.

If you are a mother, especially with kids in school, be ready to receive hearts of all kinds. Some will be homemade ones if you have children or creative husbands. Some hearts will be candy; the hard kind with cute messages written on them. Though sometimes the candied hearts get only a half-printed message so the message is difficult to read. But, it's the thought that counts, right? Oh, don't forget about the chocolate hearts...very fattening.

Besides being creative and fattening, Valentine's Day was always an exciting and special time for my kids. Our refrigerator door and the walls in the house were filled with those construction paper hearts, and any candy they received from their school party seemed to find its way into their stomachs before I could decide if it could be eaten or not. That included deciding if I could eat the candy and maybe save a few pieces for my own emergency stash or if my kids could have the candy. My kids made me feel special because I am their mother and I have always felt they are special because they are my children and not because of any ability they may or may not have. Yes, it always came back to that, thinking about Lisa and her abilities in comparison to her siblings and their abilities. I couldn't compare any of my children in very many aspects, because they were and still are very unique people. I oohed and aahed over my first born, because I was in awe, wondering how I could be so blessed to have such a beautiful baby. And, with each baby I felt that same emotion, loving each child totally and counting my blessings. I watched them grow into young adults with goals and dreams of their own and I was mindful of their progress as they worked toward those high aspirations they each had dreamed of and accomplished. I see them now as capable, smart and talented adults.

I still marvel at their different abilities, their drive, their ambition and their successes. And, I still am in awe; that I had these beautiful, capable children. I am truly blessed to be their mother.

The following was in a column in our local newspaper two years after Lisa was born. I was reassured by the poem, began to share it with family and friends and the clipping spent many years on our refrigerator.

Heaven's Very Special Child
Printed with permission of the author
Edna Massimilla

A meeting was held quite far from Earth!
It's time again for another birth.
Said the Angels to the LORD above,
This Special Child will need much love.

His progress may be very slow,
Accomplishment he may not show.
And he'll require extra care
From the folks he meets down there.

He may not run or laugh or play,
His thoughts may seem quite far away.
In many ways he won't adapt
And he'll be known as handicapped.

So let's be careful where he's sent.
We want his life to be content.
Please LORD, find the parents who
Will do a special job for you.

They will not realize right away
The leading role they're asked to play,
But with this child sent from above
Comes stronger faith and richer love.

And soon they'll know the privilege given
In caring for their gift from Heaven.
Their precious charge, so meek and mild,
Is HEAVEN'S VERY SPECIAL CHILD.

Our Ups And Downs

Years ago, when I first started writing short articles about Lisa, I thought of a good title for an article, but I didn't know how to start the story or what I would want to write, until now. I usually wrote first and then afterwards I would come up with a title that fit with the story. But, not this time. And some of the stories and titles weren't very creative, but anyway... I remembered seeing a newsletter from another state, and that newsletter had a similar name to the title I thought of. Theirs was named "Up with Downs." And I thought, "Hey, that is close to my title." (Yet, I still didn't have a story to go along with my title.) I did feel like my ups and downs were my children. Three ups and one down; cute, huh? I only say this because Lisa has Down syndrome and yes, she is cute. But more than that, it seemed like when people asked about my children they would ask about my three older children and then ask about Lisa. It was like she wasn't really a child of mine at all or that because she had a disability and was *special*, that the people questioning me about my children had to, in some way, separate Lisa from the others. I don't know, it was just weird.

In looking back, Lisa might have been one of the most consistent "Up" person of all of us. She was the one who got us up in the morning, kept us up and moving during the day and continued on a regular basis to making sure we would stay up when she had a problem sleeping.

With Lisa, I seemed to always be worried about her health and her quality of life. In those first days after Lisa was born, I wasn't sure I could handle the challenges or situations that I envisioned would occur with Lisa. I didn't know about Down syndrome and felt I was not prepared to take on what was to come. There were times when I grieved for Lisa but then just as quickly was overjoyed and encouraged by her obvious determination. My emotions swayed up and down, depending on the time, day or activity. I needed patience but sometimes had edginess instead. I sometimes felt helpless but that would gradually turn into self-reliance. These emotions were more present when Lisa was a newborn and faded over time. The fact of the matter is that all of the above happened, giving me many ups and downs to experience. But, I wouldn't change a thing; that is just how life works, I think.

The best parts of raising our kids were the 'ups' each and every day. They kept us going with their many activities and interests. During the school year, the older ones always had projects to work on after school or on the weekend and my husband and I usually had to be up and always ready, scrambling at the last minute to go buy that poster board for a sign or mix up some homemade paste because we ran out of the regular glue. You can't paste the information on the front of the poster board without glue!. They all kept us busy with weekend shuffles, figuring out who was staying overnight at whose house, when to get them the next morning and also attend those weekend sports activities in between. Later on, part time jobs and transportation also fit into the planning process and we were constantly having last minute adjustments that kept us up and about, which kept the schedule running smoothly.

There were some downs, too, but not the way you may think. The downs could be that first day of kindergarten with our oldest child. It was a downer because it was scary to let your child go off for half a day to be with a stranger and you didn't know what they did at playtime or if they liked their snack or if they took a nap. It was more of a downer with Lisa, because she was my last child to leave the nest and besides making me feel old, I felt alone in the house and nervous about how her first half-day away from me would turn out. Would she look at or talk to anyone? Would she follow directions or just sit and do nothing the teachers asked of her? Would she be happy or cry? Well, I took some time after she left that first morning to just sit and think and then I cried. She was growing up, already leaving home without me and started to learn about the mean, cruel world. But, it was not as bad as I would have imagined. She had support from the school and staff members, had people in her daily routine who cared about her and her future, and who treated her with kindness and respect. So, that downer actually was not so bad. Just me being alone in the house was the real downer.

Other down times could have also included those nights we stayed up with any one for the four children, fighting colic, fever or restlessness. The child in question would be down with whatever ailed them, and I would be up, literally all night, rocking them while they tried to sleep. Their independence was an up and down issue, as in their first full day of school, a first job or their first date. All four children kept us moving and kept us up and around, but I don't ever remember being brought down for any length of time by any of the issues before us. I just did what any mother would do and carried on. I'd say our ups and downs were just the ups and downs of raising children.

Van Rides

When Lisa was three, we were ready to send her off to her first center-based program, so she would have more interaction with others her age and abilities. Well, I *thought* 'we' were ready. Turns out, I wasn't. We did get Lisa ready, though. She had her bangs trimmed so they didn't hang down over her eyes. This was a typical circumstance for her because I waited as long as possible before I would trim them. Lisa didn't always sit still for this every other month experience, so I had to be extra careful not to nick her head with the scissors. Thus my hesitation to trim them any more often than needed. Her longer hair was neatly pulled back with white barrettes, again so her hair would not hang down over her eyes.

She wore a sleeveless dress and had on white socks with lace trim and white paten leather shoes. They had slippery soles, so I am not sure why I put those on. She looked more like she was going to church, but she looked adorable, too. She carried a large canvas bag that had two handles and the front had a picture with an array of balloons in colors of yellows, reds and blues. I had carefully marked the canvas bag with her first and last name and Lisa loved carrying it around the house. The bag was almost half her size and I wondered what she would do when any books or papers were added to the weight of the bag. She would not be able to lift it the way she did when it was empty; her dainty right wrist slightly bent and held both straps just so. We would just have to wait and see.

So, here she was on her first day of school, getting her picture taken outside our house with her siblings, as is the tradition on the first day of school each year. Then a good breakfast and a good face washing afterwards and we were ready. Well, again, I am not sure I was ready. But it was time to go. The bus wasn't actually a bus. It was a white eight-passenger van with no markings on the side to indicate it was a school bus. I knew it was the ride Lisa was patiently waiting for but I just wasn't in a hurry to take her outside. One more hug, one more check in her bag and one more hug. Ok, we were ready.

I carried Lisa outside, holding on to her tightly, as if someone might come along and snatch her. Realizing that I was carrying her, I quickly put her down on our front porch so she could proceed on her own. As we walked down the four cement steps from our house, I thought that maybe she should walk down the sidewalk to the van by herself. Start that independence thing right on her first day in a school setting. She got to the van and the driver rolled down the passenger window to direct me as to where Lisa would be sitting. So, I hurried to the van, picked her up and had one more hug before putting her in the van for her first ride away to new adventures in school. My memory has it that she ended up in the front passenger seat without a car seat, but that just couldn't or shouldn't have been the seating situation. But, then again it was the early 1980s, and I am not sure if the laws for children sitting in the front seat were in force at that time as they are now. Be that as it may, I lifted Lisa up to the seat the driver indicated to me and used the adult seatbelt to buckle her in. Ok, this is going good. A quick thank you to the driver, another hug with Lisa and then I turned around to go back inside the house. As the white van turned the corner to take her five blocks to her school, I turned towards the van and saw Lisa sitting in the front seat like a big girl, oblivious to what just happened. She was leaving home without me. But I already knew this and felt a sudden rush of sickness in my stomach and then I cried. All the way into the house and for a minute or two after I sat down. Why was that? I wanted her to go to school, to learn and grow, to be independent and someday be living on her own. So, this was the first step, but so emotional for me. I knew in my heart that it would all be ok, but at that time, in that instance when I saw Lisa in that van, all I could feel was miserable. Little did I know that my feelings would be tested time and time again, as she made her way to where she is today.

    The next time there was a van incident, I was working full-time and trying to juggle daily activities and events with the family. Lisa was in a preschool program and had an afternoon drop off. Lisa's after school sitter was always on top of things in regards to issues with Lisa, so when I received a call at work from the sitter, I knew something was up and it wasn't good. She explained that Lisa's bus never showed up after school and wondered if Lisa was home sick or the drop off plans had changed. I couldn't fathom what she was trying to tell me. Lisa didn't get to her house? How could that be? And, where was Lisa?

    This sitter had two children of her own, yet she volunteered to go drive to the school to find out if Lisa was still at the school building. I had to think about that offer for a minute, then decided it would be better if she stayed at the house just in case the van was running late and they would try to drop her off while the sitter was driving to the school. I called the school and talked to a receptionist who assured me that she would check into it to see when they picked up the children and where they were on the route. Of course, I was still at work but not really doing much work at that moment. I tried to be patient waiting for a return call saying the van was just running late, but that didn't happen. I wanted to get in my car and go find her myself, but unsure of where to go except to her school. So, I waited. Soon I received a return call from the school receptionist who had talked to the bus driver via two-way radios, and she told me that the driver said he had dropped off all the kids. Now wait a minute. Did I hear that right? If he did indeed drop them all off, where was Lisa? At someone else's house? A stranger had my child? Now my mind was racing with all types of scenarios; none of which were close to being a possible good answer. And, the driver had remarked that he did the usual last checklist routine which should have included being sure no child was left on the bus.

It was now around 4:30 and it was over an hour since the time that Lisa should have been at the sitter's, eating a snack and watching Sesame Street. I decided to leave work early. I couldn't stay and wait for someone else to find her. I had to go, immediately. I went directly to the school, which also was the last stop for the vans, where at the end of their day or route they parked the vans in a fenced-in lot to decrease the chance of vandalism. As I was getting out of the car, I saw several people over by one of the vans. My heart started to skip a few beats while it pounded inside my chest. I was afraid of what I would find when I got to the van. But, what I saw was Lisa, being taken out of the side door and she was looking fairly intact and awake.

Here's the story the school personnel could piece together. The bus driver did indeed deliver all the kids to their respectful destinations, except Lisa. He had forgotten that she had gotten on the bus and truly didn't see her when he did his last check before parking the van for the evening. But… oh yes, there is a but. He didn't follow protocol when checking the van. He did not see Lisa because she had been lying down in one of the back seats and the driver admitted that he simply scanned the seats from the front area and didn't walk all the way to the rear of the van. Really? How far of a walk could that be? Really! The school staff also surmised that Lisa had been in the van from about 3:10-4:45 with no water, no bathroom and no supervision. At some point she must have fallen asleep, because that's how they found her, asleep. They knew she had walked to the front of the van, because they realized that she had been playing with a lot of the buttons and dials on the front panel. Well, what else was she suppose to do while she was waiting for someone to remember her and to find her? I guess at this point I was getting very sarcastic and angry. This should not have happened and should never happen again. I am sure I made myself very clear on that point.

Lisa seemed to be ok. She was a little dirty with streaked, smudged tears on her face. She came to me and I held her so close and so tight that I am sure she was struggling to breath. Now everything was ok. I took her home, called the sitter to relate the story as I knew it and decided I needed to think about what to do next so that another child does not get left in a van.

The next day I call the director of the Special Education program and proceeded to tell him what I thought about the entire incident. He listened patiently and then remarked that this type of situation would not happen again. We received a letter from the supervisor of transportation services for the school district, which had an apology. He also wrote that it was very unfortunate to have Lisa on the van and not being dropped off according to the schedule. A memorandum was also enclosed that was sent to all drivers, and it is written as follows: "Beginning immediately, if there is any student left on the bus after routes are supposedly completed, there will be termination procedures initiated against the bus driver who violates this. PLEASE check your vans when you are finished with your various routes." Lisa's driver had not checked the van as he was suppose to and because of that he lost his job. Now, fast forward some ten to twelve years and we have moved three times to two different states. In Lisa's senior year of high school, this school district sent out a memo to parents of children with special needs. It was from the Director of Special Services, who coincidently had been in the first school district that Lisa attended as a baby and as a grade school student. He also remembered the incident when Lisa was left on the bus so many years before. This memo read as follows: "The following is the procedure to be followed by the bus service if a parent or guardian is not present to receive the student when transportation is required by that student's IEP. 1) The student will be kept on the bus and dispatch notified to contact the parent or guardian listed on the student's transportation request form. 2) After delivering all other riders to their stops, the driver will then return to the student's destination and see if parent or guardian is there to accept the student. 3) If parent or guardian is not at destination and dispatch has not been able to contact parent or guardian, student will be returned to the bus service office and the police department notified to pick up the student. 4) Requests for alternate drop off points and/or releases to neighbors, friends, etc. must be written by parent, be within a one block radius of the student's address, be notarized and be approved by the special needs department, with a copy sent to the special Education office."

I was impressed and a little curious. Did a child get dropped off somewhere that was not their home or was left unattended somewhere? Was there some other incident that involved a student and their safety? I never did find out what happened, but I am glad the school district was proactive in this matter. It can never be too much if it means helping those students who might otherwise have a serious safety issue arise because an adult was not present to receive that child. Lisa made it through the rest of her van-riding years without any other incidents. But, I didn't make it through the rest of her years without problems or complaints. I took on many situations and tried to make things better within the system, no mater where we lived. I was determined to always be ready.

A third van ride that comes to mind was when Lisa started at a new high school in a new town. We lived almost across town from the high school that we decided to send Lisa to, and because my husband and I both worked and there were no siblings to drive her to school, she was allowed to ride the bus. We, with the help of the special ed department, had decided this high school had more opportunities for Lisa, both in the regular classes as well as some special education supports.

I knew that the van ride would be no big deal, because she had her routine down pretty good by this time in her bus-riding years. First, get up to eat breakfast, usually cold cereal and maybe some fruit. Then, get dressed, trying to stick with the clothes that were laid out by her the night before. Occasionally she would change her mind, and then there might be some quick talking by me to convince her that the black shorts would look fine with the shirt she picked out. Once dressed, she might have time to straighten her room or comb her hair again. Otherwise, she would go outside to the front porch step, (there was only one step) and there she would sit. It might be five minutes before the van was expected or it could be 25 minutes. I tried to tell her that she could wait inside, watching from the window for the arrival of the van and be more comfortable. Nope. She always chose to sit on that step, and just sit. She didn't choose a book to read nor did she want my company.

I would occasionally watch from the window, checking on her to see if she was still sitting, and to watch for when the van would arrive. Most of the time, she waited patiently, looking around the neighborhood at any activity there might be at 7:30 a.m. Then, after a few weeks of this new van ride, in a new house, in a new town, something changed. At first, I would hear someone talking outside the front door and thought maybe a neighbor was talking to Lisa.

Nope, just Lisa sitting there. So, I put my ear up to the thick paneled, front door, trying to listen. It was Lisa, talking out loud to herself.

I called it self-talk, and in later years when I researched it, that was what professionals who know or work with people who have Down syndrome have been calling it, too. Basically, self-talk or talking to your self is how people try to work out situations that might be stressful or as an outlet for a specific activity or problem. I realize that I have heard adults, me included, who mumble under their breath, trying to say something out loud without really wanting anyone to hear. Just to hear something out loud helps to hear what the situation or problem is. I don't do it often, and in the beginning, Lisa didn't either. But, at some point, I would hear her fairly clearly and louder than in the beginning, and I was concerned about what was going on in her mind.

I was concerned enough to ask about it one morning, and she surprised me be saying she wasn't talking. So, I decided to let it go and see what would happen. The self-talk continued. I tried not to bring it to her attention of what she was doing, but I listened and then at some other point during the day, I would talk to her about that subject she had been focused on, casually chatting with her so she could share whatever she wanted to on the subject that she had visited during her self-talk time. I also tried to tell her that it was okay to talk about things when by herself, but to be aware that it might seem strange or unusual if she were in the company of others and they would not understand why she was talking out loud to herself. I never told her it was wrong or to not do self-talk, but I might have asked her quietly what or who she was talking to and if there was some way I could help her work out her problem or situation that must have been bothering her. I believed that moving to a new town and going to a new school had been the trigger for this self-talk, since I hadn't heard her doing it before this stage in her life. No teacher, nor bus driver, nor friend has ever mentioned that Lisa did self-talk and no problems arose because of it. For Lisa, it was a normal reaction and behavior for this new environment. I looked back and realized that we have had lots of different situations when it comes to van rides. These situations I have just mentioned are just a few examples.

High School

Moving kept us all on our toes, preparing all the children for a new town, new friends and a new school. The oldest was now off to college and Lisa's brothers were able to make friends easily, but Lisa took longer to adjust and make new friends. When we moved her during her sixth grade year, the changes were less challenging because we planned ahead, had correspondence with the students and teachers and tried to make the transaction as smooth as possible. Lisa was always quiet and reserved, so others had to step up to help her in the process of making new friends. Apparently, when she moved on from eighth grade, which was considered middle school at that time, to ninth grade at the high school building, she had some friends. They didn't come over to the house or ask her to go to the mall on Saturdays, but they came through in great ways. One time was at the beginning of basketball season and Lisa wanted to go see a game at the high school. Her brothers were going, but they didn't want to have to watch Lisa and that was understandable. I told Lisa I would take her and pick her up afterwards, because she said she did not really want me to actually be there with her. Here she was, being a typical teen. No self-respecting high school student would want their parent with them at a school function.

The time was set when I would pick her up and I had made sure she knew what side of the building I would be at when the game was over. When the time came, I drove over to the high school and parked where I could see the door Lisa was suppose to come out. I waited and I waited. No Lisa. Now I started to panic just a little. Ok, well maybe a lot. I was trying to give Lisa some room to grow, do things she wanted and try to handle it on her own. Oh, how I wished at that moment that I had gone with her to the game, but really, how many ninth graders have their parent sitting with them if friends were around. As far as I knew, no ninth grader would.

So now I had to figure out where Lisa was. I got out of the car and walked to the building. I walked inside to see if I could find her. I asked others, students and adults, if they had seen Lisa. At this time, I don't think she was well known at the school, but I had to ask. I tried to refrain from saying she had Down syndrome, but that was one of her most obvious characteristics, so that was part of my description of her. Nope, no one saw her. It was at this point that I wondered, "Now what do I do?" My answer came to me when I walked back outside and saw a young girl that I knew was in Lisa's grade. She told me that several of their mutual friends had decided to give Lisa a ride home. What? Lisa went with strangers? In a car? Now, you should know that I usually jump to the worst conclusion in these types of situations, and I did. I did not have a good picture or frame of mind for what I thought would happen next. And, I didn't know what to do. So, after calming myself down, I decided to go home and see if she was there. If so, all was well. If not, then I had already decided to call the police. The drive back to the house was nerve wracking for me, because there was a lot of traffic after the game, and I couldn't find a side street to get me home any faster than what the regular traffic would allow. I reached the house, jumped out of the car and ran inside calling Lisa's name. No answer. Again I though, 'Now what do I do?'

It was at about this time that I saw car headlights and the car was just turning into our driveway. I thought that it was one of the boys and I thought that was good because I could send them out to see if they could go back to the school to find Lisa or to find a teacher that could help us in locating Lisa. It wasn't the boys, but it was Lisa, with her friends. The story goes that as the game got over and the students were walking outside, one of the friends had a car and offered Lisa a ride home. Of course, I was thrilled that they asked and that she felt comfortable going with them, but I was also upset because she and I had decided on a time and place for me to pick her up, and I didn't know that she chose another way to get home. I don't know that any of the girls had a cell phone at that time, so they probably didn't think anything of their invitation to give her a ride home. I didn't scold Lisa, but tried to talk to her about how she needed to stick with the plan we had or call me to ask about making a change. It all turned out okay, as it usually does, but it sure made me a nervous wreck.

Lisa had been making friends at every new school she attended over the years and then missing them when we would have to move on. When Lisa was going into tenth grade, we had to move to another town. We tried to do some preparations ahead of time with the new school and teachers, and Lisa was able to visit the building ahead of time to see the classroom and building layout. This high school had two large buildings and as it happened, Lisa had a couple of elective classes in one building and all her other classes in the second building. So, every day she would have to walk about a quarter of a mile between buildings to get to her classes.

I was concerned about how this would work out, but she had help from some of the classmates in the beginning and then she could travel that distance in a timely manner, most of the time. This was a new experience for her and she handled it well. The bonus was: friends. Most of these friends were people with disabilities who were in some of the same classes as Lisa, but there were some regular ed students who Lisa ended up having as friends at school. Again, there was never any interaction outside of school like trips to the mall or sleepovers, but Lisa was ok with that or at least she didn't share with me that it was a concern of hers.

We lived fairly close to the school, a mere five or six blocks, so many times Lisa would walk to school. The neighborhood students knew Lisa and helped her cross the busy intersection that was the entry to the high school. When I would attend a basketball or football game with Lisa, her classmates stopped by, said hi and would maybe chitchat a few minutes. High school students do chitchat, don't they?

Lisa also had a real boyfriend at this high school. At the last town we had lived in, Lisa would tell me about a certain boy in school whom she liked and that he worked at a grocery store. So, invariably we would have to frequent that store and she would walk around looking for him. Sometimes he would be working and I would watch Lisa walk by the young man, but she would never say a word to him. I think it was a one-sided romance, but it was cute just that same. At this new high school, the young man that Lisa started to like was in a couple of her special ed classes. His speech was not very good and I had trouble understanding him at times, but Lisa caught on to it quickly and would decipher conversations for me. The two of them would go to each other's houses to visit on a Saturday or Sunday and usually just watched TV. Once or twice I remember they went out to eat and they went to a couple of school dances together. And so it began…dating!

That was cool. It was neat to see her get excited about going dress shopping to pick that perfect dress to wear, trying on shoes to match and finding that right boutonniere for him to wear. I don't think they tried to coordinate their colors, but they did look good together. Their first dance/date together I learned something that I filed in my memory banks for the next date they might have. He was afraid of balloons. For this special date, when they got dropped off at the school, they found out that the gymnasium was decorated with balloons. I got a frantic call from Lisa and I could barely understand her. So, I went to the school to find out what was going on that put Lisa into a panic. Well, when I walked into the entry of the building, I could see Lisa's date sitting on a bench outside the door to the gym and there was a school staff person with him. Lisa was nowhere to be seen. I walked over to him, sat down and tried to find out what was wrong. All that was said was that he was afraid of balloons and was not going into the gym. Lisa on the other hand, who didn't mind balloons and loved dancing, was in the gym. So, that was their very first date. I think they both enjoyed themselves, despite the situation. He was a good friend for Lisa, and I think she felt like she fit right in with her other classmates when they talked about their boyfriends.

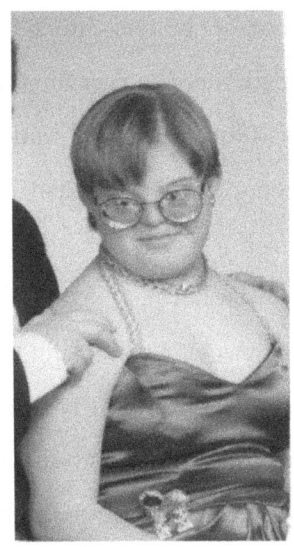

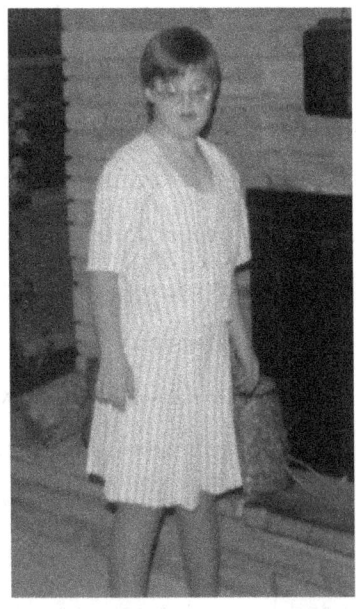

Work, Play And School Activities

Some of Lisa's classes at the high school level were challenging. Teachers were willing to have Lisa in regular ed but she spent the majority of her time in the special ed classes. This was a little disheartening to me, but Lisa seemed to do okay with the situation. When she had to go back to the special ed classroom in the high school setting, she was very capable of all that was asked of her, and then some. She actually excelled in the special ed classes and I believe it was due to her having the other school systems and teachers who helped her to keep learning all along the way through her earlier educational years. In the two years prior, she had been given opportunities at different classes; some were surprising choices as far as I was concerned. As a ninth grader, she was able to take a shop class. I don't know why she chose that, but the teacher and students helped her through that and she actually kept all her fingers intact. As a tenth grader, Lisa was able to take a weightlifting class at the school. She loved this so much that she asked if she and I could go to a workout establishment that was close to our house. I ended up doing that with her for quite awhile and I usually went with her because I had a more flexible schedule than Lisa's Dad. I tried to help her with the weights, but because I was her spotter and she could lift more weight than me, I had to insist that she not lift her normal amount of weight. We also utilized the stationary bike, a slant board for sit-ups, cables and pulleys and dumb bells. I felt like a dumb bell, because I had never done any weight lifting or exercise of this kind. But, I think it sparked something in Lisa, because with our next move to another state and town, she ended up going into weight lifting big time. But, that's a story for another time.

When Lisa turned 16, she mentioned that she wanted to work somewhere. I was not familiar with how to go about doing this, so we just forged ahead. We lived close to a fast food restaurant and I thought that might be ideal if she needed to walk to or from work. This turned out to be a great experience for Lisa. We first filled out an application and then got called in for an interview. I was able to attend with Lisa, which was helpful for both the manager and Lisa. She was still a little quiet and reserved, so I helped with some of the more difficult questions being asked. She was to be front staff, which meant she kept the tables clean, made sure there was no garbage on the floor and kept the condiment bar neat, clean and filled with all those extras like pickles, ketchup, salt and napkins. They gave her W-2 paperwork to fill out, a uniform and visor and said to start that next Saturday. She worked every weekend, Saturdays and Sundays, which worked out well because she was in school during the week. If she needed time off, they were very accommodating. Some of the staff crew trained her, which at the time didn't seem unusual to me. Later on, as Lisa got other jobs while in yet another town and school system, those establishments had to go through the schools' job training program and have a job coach for her. But with this first job, she didn't have one and obviously didn't need one. The staff and manager trained her just as they would have to do for any new hire. She was also given a chance to work in the back area, where they made biscuits and other such items that were needed daily. She loved this change in her duties, even though it didn't happen often. But it might have been the beginning of her love of cooking, because when she moved out of our house and into her own apartment, she was cooking up lots of great meals. I guess you never know how one activity will work into some other circumstances or opportunities.

After she had been working at this job for a while, she asked if she could also work at another job. I thought she meant that she wanted to quit this first job and search for something else, but that wasn't the case. Here she was, an eleventh grader with one weekend job, so I didn't know how she would work in another one. But, her answer was to work one or two evenings during the week. For Lisa that was not an issue, because most evenings she would just be watching TV or doing something with the family. We went to a grocery store that was also close to our house, but not close enough to us that Lisa could walk there. We were near some busy highway intersections and it was too dangerous for anyone to try walking across that traffic. So, I made a commitment, too. I would drive her to and from work on those evenings. Again, there were the forms to fill out and an interview, but there were no problems and Lisa was hired. She was now washing dishes, clearing tables and keeping the dining area of the food section clean in this grocery store restaurant.

Again, she received a uniform, hat and an apron with the

restaurant's name and logo on it. She was a hard worker and never complained much about all the lifting, cleaning and monitoring her work area. She had trouble with the ice machine on occasion, but then she would ask for help or tell another staff person about the situation and someone always took care of it without fail. There was only one time when she had some trouble and that was brought on by her own doing. She usually didn't wear jewelry, but had received a special ring with two small, white pearls that I used to wear but then couldn't because it no longer fit me. I had Lisa try it on and it fit, so I let her wear it. Then, she received her class ring, and now owned and wore two rings. I worried that she would misplace them but she constantly reassured me that she would be careful.

One evening, Lisa came home and was taking off her work clothes from the grocery store restaurant. She quickly came out to me to say that she didn't have her rings in the pocket of the apron. I didn't know she had worn them to work and asked her why she would do so. She said that she always worn them, took them off while working and then slipped them back on at the end of the shift. She remembered that she had to empty a couple of the trays that had a lot of trash on it and thought that maybe she tossed her rings in with them. How that would have happened, I don't know. I do know that we went back to the grocery store restaurant and talked to the manager who was on duty, who said he would keep an eye out for the two rings. We gave him a detailed description of both rings and hoped for the best. I said a silent prayer, too. The manager called the next day and told us that someone had found the class ring and turned it in, but the pearled ring was not found. I thought that was interesting; that if both rings were lost at the same time, in the same place, in the same way then wouldn't they both be found. It was not to be. I was sick about the loss of that ring, for it had some personal sentimental value to me, but I didn't say anything to Lisa because I didn't want her to be upset by the loss. And, in thinking about it I realized that if I didn't want to take a chance of it getting lost, then I shouldn't have given it to Lisa. So, it was really ME who caused the sick feeling I had from the incident.

Since then, we had to move to a new city and for a while Lisa didn't have a job. She was busy getting use to a new school, new teachers and new friends. Again. But, she managed it well, adjusted to the changes and learned from the challenges.

BARCUS

Sponsored Child

Lisa has a big heart and a small pocket book, but that did not stop her from saying yes to a request when asked to sponsor a child in the Philippines. It started when we were in church one Sunday morning. The organization, which was founded in 1981, was Catholic affiliated. After our church service, there was a speaker who talked about this program that helped families and their communities. The organization was asking for parishioners to step forward (not physically or in a literal sense) but to search your heart to see what could be done to support this worthy cause to help others less fortunate.

Lisa was 16 and in 10th grade. She also had a job, so extra money was coming in for her to spend as she wanted. She didn't spend much money; in fact, she was a miser, a frugal person and a tightwad when it came to spending her own money. She would always try to get others to buy her a treat if possible but would buy her own treat if necessary. She would also buy her extra items that she might want, like a new backpack that looked like the one Suzy from school had or that new T-shirt with her current WWE favorite wrestler or some cute animal plastered across the front of it, with sad eyes staring at whomever was trying to see the front of the t-shirt.

So here we were in church and Lisa heard the guest speaker tell about the needs in the Philippines and what could be done to help the children. After the service, on our way out of church, Lisa stopped and picked up a brochure that had an application form in it. They also included a photo of the child in need, so Lisa had carefully perused the choices before settling on an 6 year old boy whose photo showed him standing outside, in front of a bush and he was clad in loose gym shorts and a plain, non-descript t-shirt. She had all kinds of questions and we tried to answer them as best we could. More discussion continued at home, through breakfast and throughout the day. We sat down with her to discuss her money situation, which was pretty good considering she had money; enough money that she could afford the $20 a month cost and still have spending money, pretty much without having to budget. It was a go and we helped her fill out the detailed forms. I was pretty proud of her making such a commitment and at the age of 16 no less!

Every month we helped her write and send a check. That was short lived because she didn't want to write checks and just told us we could do that for her. Later on, we went and set up an automatic payment withdrawal and that worked well for almost ten years. Lisa sponsored this young man until he graduated from school and was no longer eligible to be sponsored. During all those years, Lisa was involved with choosing and sending him letters, birthday and Christmas cards plus some small gifts that were allowed. In the beginning, the gifts amounted to pencils, notepaper, stickers and other small items that might interest a young boy. And, because Lisa loved buying t-shirts, he was a recipient of a few t-shirts over the years. When he got older, it was a little more difficult to find appropriate things within the limits or specifications of the organization's suggestions.

At some point in time, Lisa started to write to her sponsored child. I recently came across a couple of those letters. I must have had her write them and then I would type them on the computer so they could be printed off to mail. It was more legible and I corrected some spelling errors, so he could understand the words. Lisa started out with the formal greeting, "Dear ... How is your summer? I won't stop writing to you. My parents are ok. I am 20 years old. I went to Worlds of Fun and I got sunburned. I am going to sponsor you until you are 20 years old." The other letter started out the same with "Dear... How is school? My mom has gray hair. My Dad is a grandpa now. We are going out of town. The driving is kind of boring at my age because it will take a long time to drive there. I just woke up from a nap. Do you take naps once in awhile? Thank you. Lisa"

Over the years, Lisa went from writing her own letters to dictating her thoughts to me about what she wanted to say in a letter. Then, I would write them down and she would sign them. I would have to ask her what she wanted to say and what specific things I could write down. From that stage, the task went to me to write him and then I would tell her what I wrote. When letters came to her from him, I would let her read them, but she would struggle with the small print and some of the longer words. So that changed and I just read them to her. Each time we changed how to do things, Lisa was part of the discussion and always given a choice like, "Do you want to write the check or should I?" "Do you want to read it or should I help you or should I just read it to you?"

She loved hearing from him, receiving photos to show how he grew and to hear of his successes and experiences, especially hearing about how grateful he was to have a sponsor who helped him so he could participate in extra activities. When he graduated from high school, he did a year of technical school, so Lisa had an option to continue the sponsorship for one more year, which she did. I don't believe she ever missed the money that she gave so willingly, and I believe she, and hopefully he and his family, gained something as well. In the beginning, Lisa was just a young sponsor helping another person. As the years went on, I would ask Lisa if I could share with her sponsored child and his family about her having Down syndrome. Sponsors were always encouraged to develop personal relationships with their sponsored friend. Now, I didn't even give it a thought to share about her having Down syndrome in the beginning of this sponsorship, as it didn't seem to be a significant bit of information. But, as I started to write the letters from Lisa to that young man, especially as he grew older, I would sign it with my name along with Lisa's and identify myself as her mother. Which led me to think that I should explain why I was writing the letters. A reply from the sponsored child and his family was very nice, acknowledging the information was received and understood and that they were glad for her support. I would occasionally write about Lisa's Special Olympic activities, but mostly I wrote general, newsy letters about Lisa and how she was doing, things she did in school and later on things about her job and social activities. When it came time to decide whether she was going to sponsor a new person or just end the support after this young boy was no longer eligible because of his age, Lisa said that she thought she had done her part to help others. My thought was and still is, that Lisa has done her part helping others by just being Lisa, learning and sharing life through her life experiences.

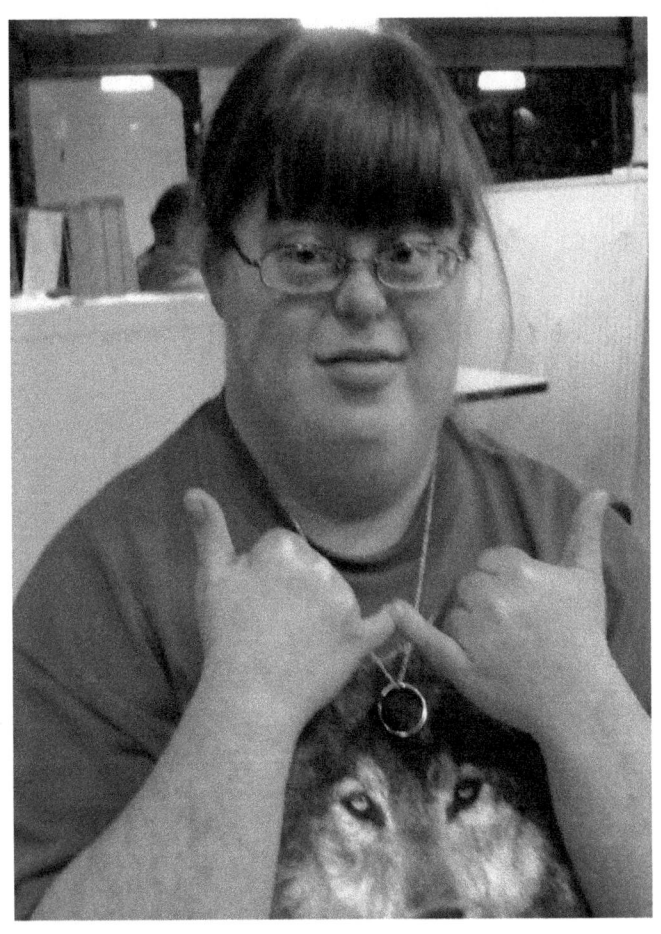

More High School

Another new school, another time to enlighten teachers and support staff about Lisa's past school failures and success, what worked best for Lisa and what we expected from Lisa and from those who would work closely with her on a day to day basis. We had looked into this school district, visited the buildings and teachers and looked at the neighborhood for a possible house to buy. Each time I thought that this would be our last move, hoping to put down roots for Lisa, my husband and myself. Each time, I had good vibes or not so good vibes about certain issues. I felt this new school district was honest in what they were telling us about the high school setting, what they believed in and how they reacted to our requests. We set up and attended an IEP meeting at the end of the school year, in May, while Lisa was still a freshman in another school, in another state. We wanted to make sure that the transition would be easy for Lisa. Getting teachers to understand what we wanted and helping them through the process should have helped in the fall when Lisa would actually attend the high school. But, I am not sure that's how it turned out. The IEP they mailed us had things written down that I questioned, like "The student does not participate in a regular physical education program," or "The student is not expected to participate in extra-curricular or non-academic activities." Huh? She has almost always been in a regular physical education program, and I would hope that if she wanted to participate in other activities related to the high school, she could *and* would. Then the IEP listed goals and objectives, but pretty much they were taken from her old IEP in the high school she was attending at the time of the meeting. I understood that the idea was to continue what she had learned at her last school and hopefully carry on what had worked, building on those skills and working on the problem issues as consistently and in earnest to help Lisa to learn and grow. But, I also thought that this new school might want to interject some thoughts or ideas of what they could do for Lisa, in addition to utilizing the current IEP information. At the end of this IEP from the new school, there was a single sheet that was a notice and consent for initial placement. In part, it read "based on that information, the IEP committee, of which you were a member, determined that proper placement is in the Self-Contained classroom." I started to fume when I read that. I know we discussed Lisa being in a regular homeroom setting and having her be in the different regular education classrooms if at all possible, but instead I had to read that she would be in a self-contained classroom. By definition, this is a classroom for children with more serious disabilities who might not be able to be in or participate in the regular education classes. Or, in some cases there might be certain students who were in a least restrictive environment (LRE) but obviously we were not able to have Lisa in a LRE classroom with this new school district. The issue about the LRE is mentioned in the Individuals with Disabilities Education Act and it is written as such to require schools to place children who have a disability in the same setting in which their regular education peers would be taught. It should be for the best interest of the child, not for what the teachers or the school think might be suitable.

There was a check mark next to an option under the heading of "other options" and what was marked said "placement in the resource room during part of the day and regular classroom placement for the remainder of the day/modified regular instruction program." Right below this typed comment, there was a handwritten note that said "We rejected this option as insufficient to meet Lisa's current needs. As Lisa transitions to the high school, this option will be reconsidered." Now, did you follow that? I had to read it and re-read it. To this day, I still am confused. Lisa was in high school before coming to this new high school and she would still be high school age there. I think what made me mad was the fact that they didn't place her where they said and where I think we all agreed to at the IEP meeting. In addition, they wrote this reasoning and all it told me was that she would probably not have much, if any, time in a regular homeroom class or other classes for that matter. And, basically that was how it started. I was so close to saying forget it, we are going to another school district, because I felt they just didn't adhere to what was agreed to as a team. But, we had already purchased a house and made plans to move right after the school year ended for the summer, so Lisa could become familiar with the neighborhood and practice walking to and from the high school before the fall session started. I suppose I felt stuck, and just hoped for the best. I also suppose that we could have still moved into that house and neighborhood, but requested a transfer to a different school district, and we would transport Lisa to that area for her schooling instead of this school district who did not follow through as I thought they would. Boy, I sometimes wished we had jumped ship right then and there, but we moved forward to an experience I will never forget. I won't bore you with how it went during her sophomore year (which was her first year at that school), except to share some comments that from teachers and staff such as "Lisa needs to ask when wanting to leave the classroom," "Lisa left class 20 minutes early," or "Lisa will serve morning detention for leaving early." These comments were few and far between and we had no indication to think that things might not be going as well as we thought. But, these remarks are important to mention here and to remember…for another story, coming up next.

Manifestation Determination

Can you say "manifestation determination" three times real fast? Do you know what manifestation determination means? I didn't until late fall of Lisa's second year at the high school she was attending. Her first year there as a 10th grader was fairly uneventful, except she didn't have a lot of classes in regular ed classrooms, but spent a majority of time in the self-contained classroom. This placement didn't help with developing her social skills nor did the teachers or other staff members ever encourage any activities outside of this setting. Lisa did make a couple of friends that were in this class and she also attended some school activities such as dances and football games.

The situation that involves the manifestation determination occurred late in the fall of Lisa's 11th grade year. She was a helper in the main office, taking notes or other such items to specific teachers or helping out other staff in the office. I believe it was part of a work-study program and she used one class period doing this, at least twice a week. It got her out of the self-contained classroom setting, where she sometimes seemed to be bored and it moved her into the main office, where she could show other adults how she could conduct herself and follow directions when asked to do something. She received the usual monthly and quarterly reports plus teacher notes occasionally that said Lisa needed improvements in the classroom setting and to work on abiding by the rules of the school. The notes seemed mundane and she seemed to be doing okay or so I thought.

I was hired as a nurse for this school district and ended up being at the same high school Lisa was attending. I thought it was a plus, but in looking back, it might have been a false sense of a security for Lisa that I was there because if I had to be gone to an in-service or for any other reason, Lisa's security blanket vanished. I believe this was part of the situation for the story that is to follow. I had gone to a conference on the east coast, but before I left, Lisa acted uneasy about me being gone.

I wasn't alarmed with her reaction, just curious as to why she was so concerned about me being away for a few days. Well, things began to make sense about Lisa's state of mind when I received a call from Lisa's Dad while I was at the conference. He said that Lisa was suspended for ten days. I completed my conference and returned home where I found a note Lisa had written me before I left, but I never received it from her until I returned. It broke my heart to read it and I will share that with you later.

Before this suspension we had received several forms and disciplinary notices, which included notes about her tardiness and truancies during this school year. They had written her up quite a few times, but we were not notified of all of these incidents, only receiving an occasional, random phone call stating what had happened on a certain day. I didn't realize how many times she left class before the dismissal bell or got up to use the restroom and

LOVING AND LEARNING

didn't return or was late to a class due to socializing during the passing time between classes. She was warned about these issues, even to the point that she might lose her work study/office aide position. Well, they didn't follow through with their warnings and Lisa continued to do as she has always done, marched to her own beat. So, this ten-day suspension was a real shock. I was also shocked when I heard what Lisa did to earn the suspension.

Here is the exact discipline notice with a description of the incident: **"Concerned that Lisa may have a knife with her as reported by another student."** Under student's comments it discloses, **"Lisa's response, 'to protect myself,' which was the reason Lisa gave when asked why she brought the knife to school."** The notice also said **"Lisa showed another student the handle of the knife and told her to stay away. The paring knife had been photocopied; all 2 ¾ inches of it. The action of bringing the knife to school was wrong. We all acknowledged that, even Lisa. She said she was scared, because of the student that was teasing her. This was the same student who also told Lisa to 'get out of here, you have a problem.' At this point, Lisa made an inappropriate gesture, and that was when the other student aggressively moved toward Lisa. A teacher stepped in to separate them, and then Lisa said she was scared. Lisa said she needed the knife to protect herself."** In Lisa's case, there were a few reasons why this happened and a few reasons that it shouldn't have been taken to the depth of repercussions that it ended up being.

And, I must remind you that I was not at the school when this occurred and Lisa said she felt threatened. We found out later that it wasn't just one day, but many times that this other student and Lisa had issues. Lisa says the other student teased her, treated her bad when the teacher wasn't looking and "flipped her off." Over the years, Lisa had been teased, treated badly and probably even bullied. But teachers and staff handled those incidents in-house and nothing escalated from the situations. The discipline notice also said that we would have to attend a mandatory meeting to discuss further discipline actions. This is when I felt the walls closing in and that I had better get more information and help before attending the meeting.

Now, I should explain what manifestation determination means. Because I didn't write down the meaning at the time of Lisa's suspension, I did an on-line search in 2016, and I came across The Center for Parent Information and Resources (CPIR) [16] that says "manifestation determination is a review to determine whether or not the child's behavior that led to the disciplinary infraction is linked to his or her disability." Under IDEA, the Individuals with Disabilities Education Act, discipline procedures required this review if a school system had to act on a discipline problem. Over the years, there have been amendments to IDEA with a simplified process in 2004. These amendments were made about seven years *after* Lisa's incident, which might have been helpful information that may have been beneficial to rectify the situation in a better way than how it was handled. I wasn't sure the determination review was warranted or necessary, but I also wondered why they hadn't started the manifestation determination process during Lisa's ten-day out of school suspension. If it would prove that her action was related to the disability, after the ten days she could have gone back to regular education classes with supports. There would have been no forty-five day suspension at the Day school nor would there have been any more OSS. (Out of School Suspensions.) The IEP team gave their reasons for delaying the determination process. "The other student would know that Lisa was back and the family would wonder what was done in ten days of her OSS. And, it would not 'look good' after such an incident to go back to the same setting so soon after the incident." I thought that the delay tactics only benefited the school and supported their safe school act and handbook. I also felt like the family should not have a right to ask or to know the disciplinary actions. But, that's just me thinking some things should be kept private.

    I thought we were ready for the meeting, having talked to many people and in gathering what I thought was some necessary information. The words manifestation determination were being mentioned and I needed to look that phrase up to become acquainted with it. But obviously, we need not have done anything to get ready because I believe the IEP team (minus us) had already decided what was going to happen. I also know that as Lisa's mother, I was to protect her and I felt I had failed. Within thirty-six hours of hearing about her suspension, I had a wide range of feelings from anger, revenge, dismay, confusion and pressure. I also felt like I couldn't trust anyone in the school district and I would cry over anything, for no specific reason. I was angry at the way the faculty handled the situation, beginning with them holding a "pre" manifestation meeting, again without us. They looked only at the fact that it was a "weapon" and what their handbook stated about weapons. They didn't address Lisa's disability, nor did they say that this was an isolated incident. There was also no mention of any circumstances that could have led up to this incident. I did agree with the ten-day suspension because Lisa did break the rules and needed to be held accountable and endure the consequence. But, the rest of it…well.

I believe she was set up to fail, for prior incidents weren't addressed nor was anything done pro-actively to discourage other problems that could arise. Lisa's teachers seemed unfazed by those missteps until the day the occurrence happened. And suddenly, I did not trust them to do what they said nor to actually say what they meant. They talked about Lisa's "behavior." Wait a minute! Taking a knife to school is not a behavior, it is an action. The behavior would be why she did what she did. I thought it was more important to ask, "What caused her to do this?" All of a sudden, a couple of teachers mentioned a well-known Day School that was for kids who had behavior problems. Since my time in the nurse's office that past year, I had heard teachers comment on certain students who had ongoing issues, and the teachers said they hoped they could write them up again, so the student would end up going to the Day school. Lisa was not a troublemaker and had no reason to be sent away to the Day School. So, in my mind, for the teachers to bring up Day School for Lisa was insane talk. Lisa's Dad and I tried to look at all the circumstances that led to this; Lisa being threatened and then getting the discipline while the other girl got to sit down and cool off. No one asked for the whole story and the stories didn't completely jive. No one knew all the facts except Lisa and the other girl. During this first meeting everyone had their notes, scripts and knew the outcome.

There was really no discussion or a plan; everything was clearly orchestrated and led to the alternative placement at the Day school. There was no discussion on the manifestation determination, even though I had tried to bring it up at least three times. Basically, manifestation determination means that the student will be tested and assessed, to see if the issue in question was related to the disability or not related to the disability. But it was mentioned to us several times that ultimately the superintendent has the final say and could still expel Lisa. So by doing the alternative placement, that would show willingness on our part and good intentions. Also, the other family was mentioned several times, saying they could possibly file charges, and it sounded like the IEP team was insinuating or threatening, as to say, you better do it this way so the other parents don't sue. During the meeting, they did address what to do if the behavior was unrelated to the disability but did not address what would happen if the behavior *was* related to her disability. They kept saying that "we decided" (which I took to mean "they decided") at the meeting to delay the manifestation determination process and said we knew that we could always go ahead and ask for it later on.

Five days into her out of school suspension, Lisa was trying to work on the ten days of homework assigned to her while she stayed at home. I felt like it was WAY more homework than she or anyone in her LD class was doing in a ten-day period, so I wrote the teacher a note explaining the difficulties. I even mentioned that if this was a true picture of what was expected of Lisa and in the time frame she was suppose to be finishing the homework in that classroom, then maybe we should revisit her IEP and what was expected as to what she could really do. With this plethora of work and Lisa at home alone during the day, she was to work on it daily. Sometimes she did pretty well with the reading assignments, except for all the writing she had to do. She was and still is a slow writer, and even back then her words were not always decipherable. With her math, she would have had to do ten pages a day in order to finish all the assignments within the ten-day suspension period. But invariably, when I returned home in late afternoon, I would review her work and then sadly have to erase a lot of it for her to redo because she didn't understand or do the problems correctly.

After the ten-day out of school suspension, Lisa was to go to a forty-five day placement at the Day School that I dreaded. Their reasoning was that Lisa should not return to the regular school setting while the determination process was being conducted, and (again) the other student who was involved would know that she was back and then supposedly this would prompt the family to wonder what could have been done in the ten-day time period. I did not believe the family had any right to ask or know the disciplinary actions. But, according to the school staff, it would not look good after such an incident to go back to the same setting so quickly. The delay tactics benefited the school and supported their safe school act as well as their handbook, which showed there was a consequence in place for the action.

When the IEP team convened for another meeting during Lisa's forty-five day suspension, her teacher from the LD (Learning Disability) classroom brought a "informal behavior intervention" plan, already written down. This teacher's notes all came from a phone conversation and several private comments between her and I. She had everything written and ready to implement, without ever telling me what she was going to do. There was no group meeting about behavior intervention strategies, just the teacher's writings, which included my comments. She had gathered lots of information for months but was just now focused on it to use in the situation regarding Lisa. The thing is that Lisa was a typical young adult. She would act or react, as all kids do, through modeling. There are lots of kids, especially in high school who flip others off, say things or act out, but do they have disciplinary notes in their files? I doubt it. Lisa's action caused her to be suspended but the other girl who had taunted and teased Lisa just got to cool off. Do I sound a bit peeved? Yup.

After this meeting, the teacher in the LD classroom came to talk to me in nurses' office. She explained the different notes she had sent, said she hoped Lisa would return to her classroom and admitted that Lisa knew it was wrong and knew that it was against the school code of conduct, but that maybe she didn't know the ramifications. This teacher said she understood how I felt as a parent. She said she was sorry if I felt side-swiped but that the form she used was new for that year and she was just practicing listing Lisa's past incidents that weren't reported, and that it was just a coincidence that she had that information for this latest meeting. The teacher also reported seeing Lisa at the Day school and that Lisa would have recreational therapy with a group and would do a physical education class with another group of students. This surprised me, since we were told that Lisa would not be with any other students, that she was to have her own classroom, teacher and basically be privately tutored. Well, I guess that didn't happen quite the way we had initially been informed about the Day School arrangements.

What I wanted to do was to go to court, sue the school and see what we could do to change the system. Lisa's Dad and I never believed that the school district did everything in the proper order or that it was even legal, at least with some of the things that transpired, but we also felt stuck. I mean, if we had hollered "due process" or other such options that were suppose to help Lisa get a fair shake, that it would prolong any action to get Lisa back to her regular school setting. And now, looking back I still wonder why I thought getting her back there would make everything better. It didn't. We decided that a better thing to do was to get her back in the regular education system after the forty-five day suspension. I also thought the faculty sounded more concerned about the other family and their welfare, trying to save face and show good faith to that other family or prove a point to us. And above all, Lisa's Dad and I would probably never sue a school district, because in the past, we had always been able to work with teachers and staff to solve any issues that came up in regards to Lisa and her schooling.

In my research to find help and answers, I came across one of my nursing books, The Merck Manual, 13th edition, which is a diagnosis and therapy medical textbook. It stated the following about mental retardation: "...Because their thinking is concrete, and they are often unable to generalize, adjusting to new situations is difficult and their poor judgment, lack of foresight and gullibility make them particularly susceptible to delinquency. Serious offenses are uncommon but the mildly retarded may commit impulsive crimes, often as a member of a group and sometimes in order to achieve peer group status." In regards to behavior disorders, it says "…and physically aggressive behaviors are usually excessive responses to normal stresses; they are often situational, and precipitating factors can usually be found." So, to me this meant that we might have a chance that Lisa's action could be seen as probable cause to why her behavior should be determined as being related to her disability.

I tried to reach out to others who might have some experience in this type of situation, such as people involved in the state and national Down syndrome organizations and Arc friends and members. I thought someone might be able to help us sort this all out. One person who was on a national board said this about Lisa and the situation, "…just the fact that she has Down syndrome as a diagnosis is enough to say that her disability did have some relationship to her action. Down syndrome is a form of mental retardation, and will be a factor in everything she does, forever. Down syndrome is a disability and a definite contributing factor throughout her entire life." According to the IEP, the most current and in most of her older IEPs, it states "In new and uncomfortable situations, Lisa is shy and avoids communications." A written goal in the IEP from the current school said that "there should be certain modifications to the states' yearly testing…so that Lisa is not required to take certain tests because of the severity of the handicapping condition." The school system knew her shortfalls in education and they didn't want her doing state tests that would probably bring the school's total average down. They had also written that Lisa had a severe case of Down syndrome, but on all other past IEPs from other schools it stated she was educable. And I was thinking, what did they mean by a severe case? She has Down syndrome. There is nothing severe, awful or terrible about that; the fact is, she just has Down syndrome.

Before the end of the forty-five day school suspension, there was another meeting. I was still feeling bad. I felt stripped, knocked down, beaten. No one wanted to listen to the circumstantial evidence, to Lisa's past history (never a threat before) or our input. At this point I was ready to walk away, get through the next few months, and 'Get out of Dodge.' The faculty still talked of the other family. Boy, that family really knew how to scare teachers. Nothing ever came of the other girl. For her, life went on without a blip. When I repeat the entire story to others, they all ask what happened to the other girl. And, I had to answer, "Hummm well, nothing." I felt like Lisa was treated poorly. The IEP team did a poor job and did whatever they needed to do to get what they wanted, no matter whom they affected.

Certain people at the meeting sat quietly and looked somewhat ashamed at the process of the meeting, but never said a word in our defense. They were not able to do the right thing and speak up about their thoughts or views on this. Lisa's classroom teacher continued to talk about whom she thought Lisa was, but that teacher was way off. She did not know Lisa. She treated Lisa like someone with a disability, someone who couldn't learn. This teacher's thinking was what I now imagine of others who live in that state where this happened and what they must think. Probably something like, "Those people with disabilities can be around, just not around me, unless they are perfect." I have never felt so bad, so frustrated and so very angry.

But by this meeting, I was ready. Not for a fight or to tell them what I thought, but I was ready for me. I brought a list of bible verses that I had looked up and they had to do with patience, understanding and forgiveness. I would look down and read one of the verses when my head was full of all that negativity and I would try to focus on the good. The meeting was long and difficult. But, afterwards was worse. Lisa was able to return to this high school with stipulations. One condition was having not one, but two female teacher assistants (TAs) to be with her at all times, even when Lisa had to go to the bathroom. Lisa was also supposed to be responsible to be sure the TAs were with her at all times and I said it should be the TAs who were hired that should be responsible for staying with Lisa. These TAs are the paid, adult staff. Lisa should not have to be responsible for making sure the TAs were with her. But again, the teacher said it had to be Lisa's responsibility. The teacher also said that ultimately it was *her* job, (the teacher's job) which was on the line. Well then, I thought to myself, would you rather have the TAs be responsible or Lisa. This was the same teacher that just sat through many meetings saying and hearing how Lisa had *not* acted responsibly in her actions that ultimately led to her suspension. All I could think was, "Whatever."

Prior to Lisa's time in this new high school, her last school had her in a learning disabilities (LD) class mainstreamed into regular education classes part of the day…with one paraprofessional to help her when needed. It was noted at the last school that her greatest deficiency was in social skills. It was also noted that Lisa could communicate well and with confidence but that it took her a long time to open up (as long as a semester) and that she didn't know how to socialize with people. It was noted that she was well liked by peers and adults and that she was kind-hearted, but was also shy and would avoid communication in certain circumstances. Seemed strange that this current school staff didn't read any of these comments that were on her IEP from that last school Lisa attended before coming to this new high school.

    For Lisa, returning to the school was scary. There were more restrictions, more rules and more demands and I felt the school system set her up to fail. I knew that Lisa needed to carry some responsibility, but here was someone who had trouble with problem solving, she functioned between 2nd and 3rd grade level and yet was being told that she was also responsible for other adults.

    At some point the TA situation changed. They brought in a male TA to replace the two female TAs and Lisa was able to go to the different classes with him following her. She actually liked him and that was a good thing. For me, I had some changes at the school, too. I lost faith in this school system and my heart wasn't in my work. I didn't go to the cafeteria to eat, but brought a sack lunch and ate in the nurse's office. I found out that this confidential matter regarding Lisa was not so confidential. Other teachers, who had no reason and should not have been told about it, did know. One came in to talk to me about it and I was just stunned that she knew. It was suppose to be confidential, but obviously that wasn't the case. Others, who use to stop and talk to me, didn't and those who saw me in the halls didn't acknowledge me. I had decided to change jobs at the end of the school year and I also went to counseling, to rid my negative thoughts and feelings. In time, things got better.

I met with Lisa's counselor who asked about Lisa, what kind of person she was, her past history, including time in regular education classrooms, teasing situations, etc. We discussed the current situation including what I thought escalated the problem that brought on the suspension and what kind of interaction might work. She truly wanted to know what I thought, how we could do problem solving on the teasing issues and how to increase socialization skills with Lisa so she might have a few more friends. The counselor was very honest, willing to listen, heard me, offered her help to me at any time and told me that she would hold any and all information that came from both Lisa and I in the strictest of confidence. Boy, that reassured me and made me feel good.

One time, Lisa's special education teacher came in to say Lisa had a good week back in her classroom, and gave Lisa a choice of whom she would like to walk with her to her classes, her current escort or the substitute who had been helping. Lisa's comment, after she chose the substitute, was to say she had a crush on him. (Well, the hormones were still working.) Later that day, I saw Lisa walking down the hall with the adult she had chosen, and she was waving a pass at the security person who was monitoring the hallways. Lisa was very talkative and happy about her escort. He seemed to be very nice and was getting along great with Lisa. You could tell that he showed a genuine interest in whatever she was saying to him and gave her the attention she needed. All during the conversation she was smiling and she seemed very comfortable with him. I found out later that she had told him that she was going to get a ride home from me. And, I guess that made her happy, too.

After the forty-five day suspension and after Lisa went through many tests, the IEP committee gathered again to discuss the outcome of the manifestation determination results. The decision said, "to the extent to which the student's behavior is or is not related to his or her disability: Did the student's disability impair his or her ability to understand the impact and consequences of the behavior?" Yes was checked!!! Note: the team also discussed that they believed that Lisa could and did learn the school rules and could appropriately follow them. The IEP team determined that Lisa's behavior was related to her disability. A new IEP meeting was scheduled to do revisions and to include a behavior intervention plan. Notes from a Manifestation Determination report stated, "Lisa's critical thinking skills are significantly limited, and that she has not developed abstract thinking skills." Also mentioned was the fact that "she functions much like a child of about six years of age." Gee, did they read any of her IEP information that came with her when she first started at this school? (Do I sound like a broken record?) And, I disagreed with the finding that she functions at that age level, but I felt it was probably how she was tested. She had a lot of smarts and experiences that other six-year olds did not possess. But, that was a battle I was not going to fight. Lisa's Dad and I knew Lisa and her capabilities, and their determination findings didn't have the last word on her functioning abilities; at least not in my book.

Another suggestion that was mentioned was to consider

possible placement at another school...far away. HA. That was never going to happen. Send her off to some school where she can't live at home, in an area where those students with disabilities and behavior issues attend the same school. We even received a nice little folder with a brochure of the school, their mission statement, a description of the programs and a three-page list that explained the levels of mental retardation, the definitions and a lengthy part about an introduction to mental retardation. After I tried to silence the thoughts that were screaming in my head saying, "No way, not now, not never" would Lisa go there, I then pondered the terminology that was plastered all over this information packet. The word retardation need not be spoken or written anywhere, any more. We should all be saying intellectual disability or specify the disability, as in Lisa's case, Down syndrome. But there it was, all those derogatory words in a nice, neat folder that was handed to us to consider an alternative placement for Lisa. Well, that would not be the place we would have chosen, even if we thought sending her to another school would be appropriate and beneficial.

  I had been in contact with the state's Protection and Advocacy services during the time that the manifestation determination was being conducted and presented them with what information I had, what had transpired and what was being done. The following is from the state's protection and advocacy services representative: "We sent information to ---(a school staff member) because we wanted to see if there was anything we could do to make this better for Lisa and for others that come to this high school. We also wanted to make the school district aware of the obligations necessary to meet students needs, especially for students with special needs." The woman with the Protection and Advocacy service organization also wrote the following: "Lisa signed the Code of Conduct without the parents being there or knowing it was being signed. (Lisa's present levels for academic skills were stated as first to upper second grade level.) How could she have understood as any other 11th grader would have in this code she was signing? The school was at fault for not following up on earlier incidents such as leaving class early and gesturing inappropriate actions. Why didn't they delve further into what the other girl had done to Lisa that made her feel threatened? Lisa had a paraprofessional at her prior school; why not at this one? A complaint to the office of civil rights may be in order here. I believe the school has discriminated against Lisa based on her disability. The IEP did not address Lisa's needs appropriately. I see no specialized services and support in place for encouraging socialization. The IEP did not address her problems with tardiness and truancies. How are they going to help her be on time? A talking watch? Having a paraprofessional to monitor hall behavior from a distance? There was no adequate transition plan for Lisa. What about self-advocacy help? Or vocational plans? Do they have any formal plans for any of the above mentioned issues?"

    Also enclosed was a ten-page form that was a child complaint process that we could fill out if we felt the educational rights of our child was being violated. This letter and form came to us after Lisa's forty-five day suspension and after she had another six weeks or more back at the high school with the TA support and some changes to the IEP. And, had we thought Lisa would be attending that school the next fall, I may have considered filing a complaint. But, guess what! We were moving again. And, this was a good move because we knew we had to get out of this state, town and high school district, and where we were going would hopefully be just what we all needed.

Remember I mentioned a note I found at home from Lisa, sometime after I got back from the conference. On the front she wrote: "NO NO NO NO! Don't go. Inside: Dear mom, Hi mom don't go don't go what did I do? All I do is love you, if you go I will cry. I like being with you. I will always look up to you. I love you. Your true love, Lisa m B." I wish I had seen that note before I left for the conference. Maybe I wouldn't have gone. Maybe none of this would have happened. I guess we will never know.

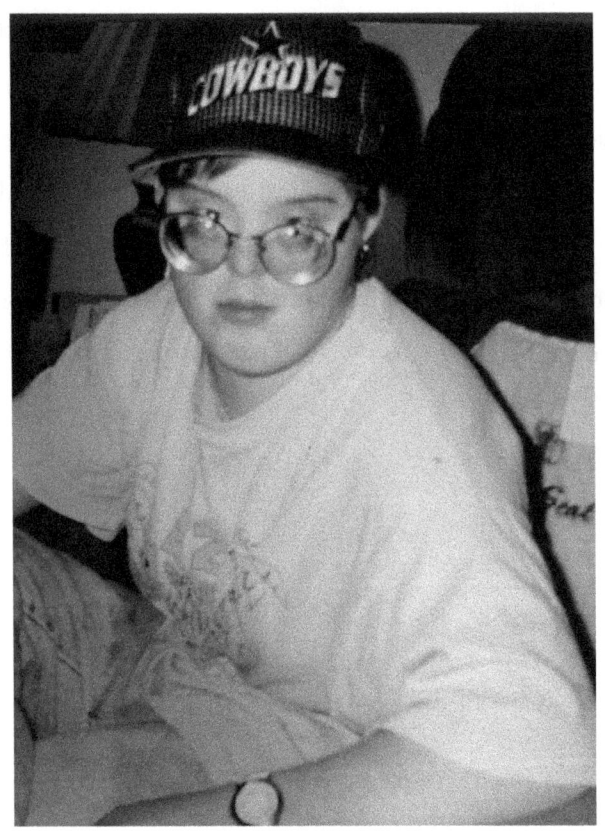

Guardianship

After the whole fiasco with the school district and Lisa's troubles due to bringing a paring knife to school, I felt that we had to protect Lisa in some way for her future. If the school district had pushed the issue during the manifestation determination process, they would have had every right to have Lisa expelled because she had signed the school's code of conduct form. This came up in conversation enough times to make me more concerned about Lisa signing things that she didn't understand or agreeing to something without knowing the consequences. So, when we received an official letter from the director of special services of the school district, we decided to look into what this official letter meant to us. The content of the letter was in regards to transfer of parental rights at the age of majority, meaning when Lisa turned 18. At that time, that meant six months from the date of the letter that we received, she would be considered old enough to become the educational decision-maker and she, not us, would receive all notices about her schooling, IEPs and other pertinent educational information. This was part of the Individuals with Disabilities Education Act (IDEA) that stated the parental rights would be transferred to the student unless the student was declared incompetent by a court of law and that a parent was appointed guardian by the court. This was one of the only times that I was thankful to this school district for sending us an official letter dealing with Lisa and her education. So, we started to look into our options. We contacted a lawyer to find out what we needed to do next. The lawyer's explanation made me sad because basically what we had to do was declare in a court of law that Lisa was incompetent and incapacitated, so that we could become her guardians. According to the Family Law Self-Help Center: "Guardianship means obtaining the legal authority to make decisions for another person. A 'guardian' is the person appointed by the court to make decisions on behalf of someone else. The person over whom the guardianship is granted (the child or the adult) is referred to as the 'ward.'" [17]

From the Special Needs Alliance site: "A guardian is appointed by the probate or surrogate court for an incapacitated person (sometimes called a 'ward' or 'respondent') and the guardian can be in charge of some or all of the personal affairs of the incapacitated person. In some states however, a person called a 'conservator' deals with the financial affairs of a person separately from the guardian. Therefore, in a case where an incapacitated person has assets that need to be protected and invested, it may be that both a conservator and a guardian are appointed for the person. In most cases, the guardian and conservator are the same person." [18]

"Normally, parents have the legal right to make decisions for their children and adults have the legal right to make decisions for themselves. Sometimes this is not possible and someone else needs to step in to take care of the needs of a child or an adult. A 'general guardianship' may be needed over an adult if the adult is incompetent, meaning the person is unable to take care of himself or herself due to mental illness, mental deficiency, disease, or mental incapacity. A 'special guardianship' may be needed if the adult is of limited capacity, meaning the person can make some, but not all decisions necessary for his or her own care." [19]

We had to prove that Lisa was incompetent, which would be difficult for me, because it went against everything I had ever thought about Lisa. I knew she was bright, intelligent, smart and capable. But, to be sure she was protected from other such incidents like the school situation, I knew that was what we needed to do. For Lisa's future and for obtaining guardianship, we had to gather all that we could to make such a statement about Lisa. It took about three to four months of phone calls, letters and requesting information to get things ready for the court date. For the lawyer, we sent Lisa's current psychological, educational and disciplinary reports that we had from the school district. We wrote to the hospital where Lisa was born to get the needed written reports and birth information that specifically mentioned that she had Down syndrome. We notified the diagnostic specialist for the school district to ask them to provide records in regards to Lisa's school information. We met with the attorney who would be presenting the case, to discuss what would be said and what questions might be asked of us and how the standard procedure of a case like this might play out.

Lisa received several papers about different items. One was a notification that a petition had been filed in the Probate Division of the Circuit Court, and that the petition would seek the appointment of a guardian for her. It said that the court was satisfied that there was good cause to exercise its jurisdiction as to the matter and a hearing was scheduled. Another official letter was in regards to an order appointing a special process server, which just meant that the court appointed a person to serve the notice to Lisa. A third letter noted that there was an order of appointing an attorney and for inspection of records. Basically, this letter explained that an attorney was appointed to represent Lisa and that appointee would be allowed to inspect and copy all records, including medical records on Lisa.

Then there was the notice of hearing, which was sent to all those people we had to list in the 'consent to appoint' form we filled out. This list included Lisa's Dad and myself. It also mentioned any and all relatives that we thought might be considered a close relative and any person who might have the power to act in a fiduciary capacity if necessary. According to Wikipedia, fiduciary is usually talking about a person who has a legal or ethical relationship of trust with someone, and that fiduciary usually takes care of money or other assets for someone else. That person should have no conflicts with the person that is being helped nor should the fiduciary collect any money or other such profits because of the position of fiduciary. The list for those who we notified in regards to the upcoming hearing included many people, not just one person.

We knew that the list of witnesses were mostly family members except one. That other person listed as a witness was the diagnostic consultant who was intregal when the evaluations were conducted for the purpose of the manifestation determination while Lisa was serving her forty-five day school suspension. I think Lisa's long history of the different school districts' records and the fact that she had Down syndrome were enough for the judge to deem that Lisa needed a guardian. So, the date was set and we thought we were ready for this. Lisa was seventeen and a half when we started this process. Time passed quickly, and too soon there were only two months with which to get it done. The official petition said, "Lisa is unable by reason of a genetic disorder since birth (Down syndrome) which impairs her abilities and has resulted in low IQ results and moderate mental retardation. Specifically, the genetic disorder causes the Respondent to be unable to receive and evaluate information or to communicate decisions to such an extent that respondent lacks capacity to meet essential requirements for food, clothing, shelter, safety or other care such that serious physical injury, illness or disease is likely to occur. That respondent, by reason of the conditions described above is unable to meet respondent's essential daily needs of living without supervision and that there are no less intrusive alternatives to guardianship available to provide for respondent's care."

All those impersonal words to describe Lisa and those words were nothing like what I might say when describing Lisa to someone who doesn't know her. I would say Lisa never gives up, is easy going, a hard worker, has a great sense of humor, is brave, determined, independent, is thoughtful and understanding. (And that is just the beginning of her list of attributes!) The day finally arrived when we went to court. I don't believe I was ever in a real courtroom and it was a little unnerving. To the left was a table where the attorney was sitting while Lisa, her Dad and I sat behind the table in some straight back, cushioned chairs. I think we explained to Lisa that what we were going to say is what was written in the latest school IEP, but that we didn't believe all of it. We explained that it was important to have guardianship for her so that people in the future couldn't take advantage of her, by getting her to sign stuff without a parent or other adult reviewing the papers first. The judge heard from the attorney, the diagnostic consultant and then Lisa's Dad and I. I don't know how he felt, but I remember sitting up near the judge and trying my best to answer the questions being asked. Some were about Lisa's abilities, her needs and possible future after high school. But, the worst part was when I had to say that she was incompetent and needed someone to be in charge of her affairs. I was on the fence with this comment because I did not, never did and still do not think she is incompetent. She had some lag in her educational needs and she would always need some help in some areas, and to me incompetent was too harsh a word. But, when I looked up the word later on, my old school Merriam-Webster dictionary said the incompetent was 1. Not legally qualified; 2. Inadequate to or unsuitable for a particular purpose and 3.a. Lacking the qualities needed for effective action and 3.b. unable to function properly, such as incompetent heart valves. It was also noted that by the simple definition of incompetent, it meant lacking necessary ability or skills. Well, I guess in some cases Lisa truly did lack some qualities or was inadequate in some situations. So, those words sounded better than her being incompetent.

At the Family Law self-help center site they state: "A guardian is appointed by the probate or surrogate court for an incapacitated person (sometimes called a 'ward' or 'respondent') and the guardian can be in charge of some or all personal affairs of the incapacitated person." [20] In our case, Lisa's Dad and I were both named as guardians for Lisa, and by our individual nature and strengths, we split the duties for helping Lisa. Because I had a nursing background, I handled almost all of her health related issues, making sure she had her medicines and took them correctly, setting up and taking Lisa to doctor appointments and dealing with the medical billing issues. Lisa's Dad was better at dealing with the finances, watching her income and outgo of monies, helping to pay her bills and keeping track of other such issues. He and I work as a team and share the duties of being Lisa's guardians. Lisa's Dad also had to fill out forms to become her payee, since only one person can be appointed to do that. When we die or decide to turn over these positions, one of Lisa's siblings will be in charge of her medical and personal situation, while another will be in charge of her financial needs. This has been designated as such in our wills.

Also, from the Special Needs Alliance site: "The appointment of a guardian for a child with a disability is one of the more important estate planning decisions a parent can make. There should be considerable discussion within the family as to who should be the guardian, not based on which other child is the oldest or who is living closest, but more importantly, which is the most suitable person to serve, who will best attend to the care and protection of the child if the parent is not living. While there is no substitute for a parent, and there is no one who will take the job as seriously and diligently as a parent, one must nevertheless consider who will be the best possible substitute to serve." [21]

There have been several incidents over the years when I was glad that we were Lisa's guardians. One such episode dealt with Lisa's verbal agreement over the phone to donate money for a fund drive. It was quite a bit of money, especially with her financial situation, as she hardly ever had any money. So, we called the establishment, explained her situation of her having a disability and that we were her guardians. This organization didn't collect any money from Lisa, nor did they ever try to contact her again. Another time, a company asked Lisa to sign some papers allowing them to bring her a product and then they would bill her, but she told the person in charge that she had to ask us first. Which I thought was smart thinking on her part, and rightly so because we did not think that it was necessary for Lisa to own the product the company was trying to sell her.

Lisa knows that we would never force her to do things that she didn't want to do, nor would we ever say that we wouldn't sign something that would allow her to do or get something she wanted. Granted, we might discuss the situation with her, come up with other options that might be a better alternative and come to a general consensus on the topic at hand. We always encourage her independence, her freedom, her individuality and her self-determination. But, we also want her to be safe, secure and protected against the ways of the world. We feel that being her guardians has been a good fit for everyone.

A couple years after we had gone through the process and we legally became her guardians, I came across an old list that was entitled "My Rights." I am sorry to say that I do not know where it came from or who wrote it, but it got me to thinking that while we were legally Lisa's guardians, we have never forced her to say, do or live any differently than what she wanted. We knew going into this legal process that she had rights and we were going to be sure that we didn't infringe on her rights. This list says it all.

"I have the right to: Live where I want; have the kind of job I want; Pick my friends and enjoy their company; Enjoy my favorite activities when I want; Attend the church of my choice; Pick who I live with; Have personal possessions and personal space; Be treated in a respectful manner; Set my own schedule; Earn and spend my own money and to really control it; Pick my own doctor and stay in the comfort of my own home when sick; Be treated fairly and not be taken advantage of; Be mad and happy whenever I want; Eat and drink what and when I want to; Make an occasional mistake; Be liked/loved for who I am as an individual; Give and receive physical affection; Spend time with and to communicate with my family whenever I want; Have opportunities for new experiences; Have both good and bad habits; Live by my own moral standards; Choose my own clothes and wear what I want; To say NO without explanation."

To me, having guardianship does not mean a person's rights are taken away or to restrict a person's freedom. I believe in Lisa's case, it is a way to help and protect her; a safeguard for her. If there are major decisions to be made, as her guardians we are able to do so. Such decisions might include medical care, living arrangements or financial concerns. She can comprehend and do things for herself, but she may not fully understand the consequences for signing certain forms when there is a major decision to be made. I believe in my heart that we made the right decision for Lisa and have still allowed her to exercise her wishes and rights.

One More High School

We moved to a new city and state after the manifestation incident, and began to settle in to getting Lisa ready for her senior year of high school. She adjusted well in the new classroom with others who had developmental or intellectual disabilities, but also adapted quickly to the regular ed classes that she was enrolled in. Lisa had to learn where all the classrooms were, which door to go in and out of to get to the other building where she had a computer class and then where to go when she needed help, such as the nurse's office, the front office or back to her homeroom class.

This transition was handled efficiently, with the high school staff and resource room staff coming together to discuss what Lisa's needs were and what would be the best classes that would benefit her as she prepared to graduate and move on to the next steps, living in the community, having a job and being a contributing citizen in every way. Because Lisa transferred in from another school in another state, an IEP update was in order. Before we attended the IEP, I had asked Lisa if she had any questions for the team and at that time she said she didn't. But, when we were actually at the meeting, Lisa produced a few questions that we tried to address as best we could. She asked the following: How do I get a boyfriend? How do I get new friends? How do I get along with others? Where is my locker? How do I get over my nerves? How do I become popular? Wow, I realized that Lisa had given my question a lot of thought and by her wanting to share her questions with others I realized that she was serious and in tune to what the IEP was all about, which has always been to help Lisa to reach certain objectives and goals. Now, I am not sure I remember how they responded to these questions, but I do know that they tried to answer them as honestly and accurately as possible. Maybe the boyfriend question was skimmed over, but in getting along with others and making new friends, I am sure the school staff gave answers that would go along with what might work in the school setting.

At some point in this last year of high school, Lisa had filled out a 12-page form, with an assortment of information, questions and comments for Lisa to ponder. Under the first section, there was multiple choice that listed "things I like about myself." She marked that she could cook well, was good with children, that she could use a computer, was great at telling jokes and was happy. The space to fill in about something to be proud of had Lisa writing that she was going to go to college some day. (I know she mentioned wanting to go and I didn't realize that she was really serious about it, but by stating this bit of information in such a positive way, I knew she meant it.) Under a new skill she learned, she wrote that she could budget and use the stove and oven. The page on making decisions, with or without help was enlightening. According to Lisa, on her own, she could decide what to eat, when to do laundry, when to go to bed, who to date, how to wear her hair and what to do on the weekend. She marked that she could use some help finding a job, and she marked that she could decide where to live on her own, and then she also added that she would need help with the living arrangements. She wrote that she wanted to live by herself, have services provided by a local organization, work at a big chain grocery store, and for fun, she would go out with friends, date or just paint her toenails. I think this gave the adults some good reading material and clear, helpful information on what Lisa wanted in life.

Lisa completed her high school years and graduated with her class. And not just with the resource room class she attended, because in that class there were different grade levels, so those students didn't all graduate at the same time. As a senior, Lisa received a cap and gown, walked into the gymnasium with her 12th grade classmates, all 300+ students that year and received a diploma for finishing her schooling. Granted, the diploma wasn't signed, but it would be after she completed two more years in another setting, which would help her with her daily living skills. In Lisa's case, as with all those students in Lisa's special ed classroom, she was allowed to have two more years of school or until she turned 21. There was a time when students with developmental disabilities from age 18 to 21 just stayed in the high school setting so they could continue to receive services. At some point, a few colleges started to provide postsecondary programs for those students who wanted to continue their studies in a setting other than the high school. Lisa had an opportunity to continue her studies through a program in this school district, but not in the high school or college setting. There were others who may have chosen to leave the high school setting to pursue a job and not take advantage of those extra two years of schooling that was available. As long as the IEP was regularly reviewed and updated, a student qualified for special education up to their 21st birthday.

During her senior year, the vocational personnel had been taking Lisa to different sites for some trial experiences working in the community. The resource classroom had a program set up that gave students a chance to see what kind of a job they might like to do after they graduated. This was treated like a real job and Lisa had a job coach who would help look for a job in the field of interest that Lisa had said she might like. This job coach also helped Lisa at the job site, showing her the different tasks she was to complete while at the work site and to give her guidance and support while she was doing the work. Lisa did a variety of different jobs in the course of that last school year, including such things as sacking groceries at a small, neighborhood store, stocking shelves, doing laundry at a hotel and working at a college campus cafeteria. A variety of skills were tried to see what worked best for her physical abilities and what she might like to do.

Since Lisa was nineteen when she finished high school, she was able to continue with her studies but in a different setting. The program was considered a community transition program and Lisa was able to be a part of it for 2 years. Because of the change in placement, there was an IEP update for new teachers to follow. Of course, some things never seem to change on her IEP, like her ability to communicate, especially to establish eye contact and respond quickly. Lisa usually had/has a lag time between when she was asked a question and when she would begin to answer it. It has been an ongoing attribute, and Lisa's Dad and I seem to think it is part of her processing technique. She hears the question, then reviews it again in her mind, decides the correct answer and starts her response verbally. If you don't give her enough time to think and instead ask a different question or shorten or lengthen the original question asked or even if you are just repeating the same question with inflection, Lisa is then somewhat stymied. And it takes her longer to decipher what she wants to say. So, the best thing to do is to wait patiently and give her time to answer the original question. And you would be pleasantly surprised at how great her answers are. Usually, on the mark and said with conviction.

Another issue brought up during this IEP was something from the last high school she attended, where issues were SO different than at any other setting, before or after that horribly long, time span Lisa had to spend in that school district. This specific comment noted that "in the past, when Lisa was unsure of herself in activities where she was more on her own, she would often choose to 'flee' the situation rather than seek help or clarification." It was clearly noted in the most recent IEP update that the current teachers and staff had not observed the problem with Lisa "fleeing." And under this new IEP behavior intervention plan, which was initially carried over from that last high school, it was noted, "behavior is not a concern for Lisa." Boy, this just reinforced the idea with me that the last high school was the problem, not Lisa. Just that quickly, we had the IEP updated and things in place for Lisa to attend this community based transitional program. Now, let's get her graduated so she can attend this great two year, after high school program.

Lisa was a part of this high school's senior class and was able to enjoy what all seniors go through when anticipating their graduation. She already had her senior class ring, which she wore all through her senior year of school. She had senior picture day, to have that one perfect photo for the yearbook. She wasn't nervous about the photo shoot, nor was she too interested in having different background settings to choose from. Her clothing was typical for her and not some fancy, dress-up attire. She didn't visit colleges because we knew she would be attending the two-year transitional program instead. She picked up her cap and gown and we made sure they fit, especially the gown. With her short stature, I wanted to make sure that she could walk up and down stairs and across the stage floor without slipping. She had senior announcements made up and sent out to friends and family. And, then we worked on the best part of graduation, the party.

When graduation day came, I was a bit overwhelmed. I had always hoped and dreamt of this day, and all of a sudden (19 years went by fast) there we were, getting Lisa dressed and ready for the walk across the large stage to get her high school diploma. Family attended, sitting up in the bleachers of this enormous gymnasium, waiting and watching for Lisa to walk by us on her way to a grey folding chair somewhere on the gymnasium floor, in the throng of seniors that were filing in. With everyone in a black gown, it was a little difficult to see Lisa. There were different colors of sashes, depicting certain academic achievements, so that helped us when looking for Lisa. It also didn't help that she was shorter than most seniors and could have been hidden between two tall classmates. It was a large class, and the procession was long as they walked from the gymnasium double doors, around the entire gym floor and then finally being directed to their specific row to sit down for the ceremony. Even though I had helped pin her cap on with about twenty bobby pins, making sure the tassel stayed on the right side of her face and her gown had been adjusted in length by me so she could walk with ease, when I saw her I was almost in tears. There she was, walking proudly and keeping up her pace with the others, all the while looking around in the crowd for us. She looked so grown up and happy. This was one of her goals from WAY back. I think in fourth grade she voiced her resolve to "graduate from high school, get a job, have her own apartment, and have a cat." Well, she was on her way to obtaining all those goals.

With such a large class, it took a couple of hours for the speeches and academic awards to be mentioned. Then came the diplomas. Even with the large number of students, in the scheme of things, we didn't have to wait to long before we saw Lisa's row of students stand up simultaneously and move forward to the stage. I guess that is one good thing about having a beginning letter of a last name that is early in the alphabet. There she went, walking up the steps, waiting until her name was called and then gracefully made her way to the middle of the stage where teachers and staff were ready to hand out the diploma and give handshakes over and over again to the many seniors in attendance. Lisa did great. No slipping or falling. That was a good start. She also remembered all the instructions from her teachers; grab the diploma with the left hand, shake hands with all the adults with the right hand; get to the other side of the stage and find the stairs to step down; get back to the correct folding chair; move the tassel to the left. She did it! I had no doubt that she could or would. She had been practicing it at school and at home and had the confidence that all would be fine. We waved and clapped loudly as she made her way back to her chair, but I am not sure she saw us. But, we waved and clapped just the same. After the graduation was over, it was time to head home for more fun.

We arrived back at the house to greet family and friends who were able to attend this very special day. The large, colorful plastic banner that was tied across half of the garage doors had the word GRADUATION plastered across it in big, bold letters. There were cars and trucks parked along both sides of the street and up the side street as well. We heard laughter and joyful comments as we walked up the back stairs to the deck, where people were already gathered with a snack and a beverage. This was such a great sight to see all those who supported her and our family over the years, as we all worked towards getting to this special day in Lisa's life.

Several who attended that day pleasantly surprised me. One special person was the teacher from her grade school years. This teacher had Lisa in fifth grade and once she realized that Lisa was to be treated like any other student and not given any special consideration, the teacher and Lisa got along great. This was the same teacher who asked to have Lisa in her classroom when Lisa was in sixth grade. This teacher had been moved up to the sixth grade classroom setting and she just felt it would be great to work with and instruct Lisa for another year. I thought maybe this teacher would send Lisa a card, but to drive over five hours to attend the party was more than I expected. And, I think they made it a day trip, leaving after a couple hours to be sure they could get back to Nebraska before it got too late for them. Her husband and her younger child had come along for the day and I think they all had a good time.

Another person who was at the house was a friend of one of Lisa's brothers. This friend had been around the family gatherings throughout the years while we lived in Nebraska, and as we moved to different states and houses, he was there for other family gatherings. He proudly stood next to Lisa with his arm around her, while photos were taken. They had a little friendly banter between cameras flashing and pictures being taken, and I could see that Lisa felt comfortable in having him at the house party. Others who couldn't attend surprised Lisa with cards, money and even a savings bond or two for the future, so she could cash it in later on, when she needed the money.

There were lots of sandwich fixings, sides and chips, cake and ice cream. Watching Lisa eating the cake made me teary-eyed, because it reminded me of her first birthday. I had been thankful that she survived her first year, thankful for the news that she didn't need any heart surgery, thankful that I was her parent and that she was a part of our family. Looking at her with my eyes wide open, watching her eat the chocolate and yellow marble graduation cake, I was also thankful for where we were in this stage of Lisa's life, now being able to look again to a future for Lisa in whatever avenue she took as she went out into society and the community as a productive, successful adult. The first adventure, the transitional community based program.

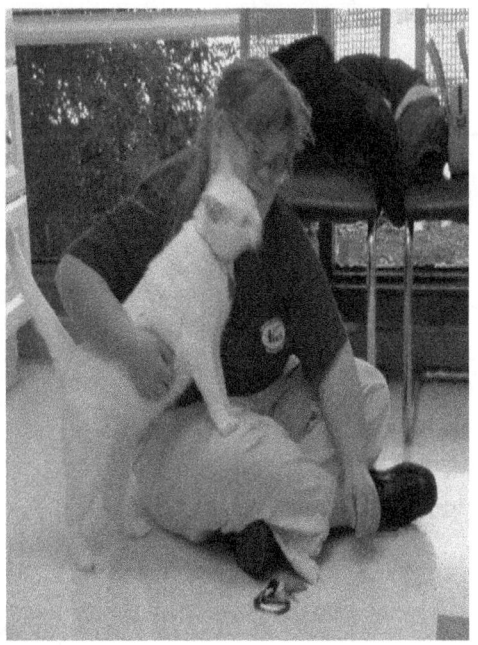

A Great Transition

Once she had her high school days behind her and fall came about, Lisa went to her new school setting, which turned out to be a two-bedroom, fully furnished, red brick duplex. The idea was to give students a true experience of living in the community, while still having the necessary supports through the school system. Part of the eligibility conditions for this program were that the student would graduate from high school, be at least eighteen years old and need continued support due to the extent of their disability.

While Lisa was a part of this program, some of the objectives and measurable goals written on one of her progress reports included identifying different coins and telling what the combined amounts would be, figuring out groups of items at different costs and totaling the amount, making sure she has enough money to buy a specific item, work on writing a check, take telephone messages legibly, address an envelope correctly and filling out forms with information where she might have to find out those answers by asking other people or researching specific documents. Some of her progress reports showed that she could do most of the above-mentioned daily skills, sometimes with help, such as using a calculator or asking another person. Other progress notes stated that she needed more assistance, that she didn't always have the opportunity to work on or master a specific goal in a normal, situational setting such as at a grocery store, or that she was still working on mastering a specific goal.

She had two years to work on her skills at "home," meaning this duplex, and in a work setting. At that time, she was still living with us and in my mind she already did a lot on her own. She had learned how to do her laundry as early as her freshman year in high school, so she was pretty good at sorting, choosing load sizes and adding soap or softener. She was always expected to make her bed and did so most of the time. Of course, I might go in and straighten it up a little and I did help her with changing the sheets, because it was what I did, always being a mom, I guess.

She was also helped in the area of social skills and getting along with others. The workbook she brought home had the sub-title "Responding to Teasing." [22] The pamphlet was unique in that there was a three-fold page at the beginning, because this would be utilized to hide the answers after the subject matter was reviewed and while the student was writing the answers in the workbook as he or she remembered them from the lesson. It worked pretty slick. Lisa learned about body language and how to respond to the teasing in different situations. The sixteen pages reiterated the information in different ways, and Lisa's answers were written in appropriately throughout the booklet. Lisa's quick-witted written response to a question at the end of the booklet was the best, as far as I was concerned. The statement was about if she had encountered teasing at home or in the neighborhood, and asked who might be that person who would tease her. Lisa's answer: Adam. (That's her brother!) And, yes it is true that he would tease, just a little more than the other two siblings. It is part of what this family does in a friendly banter kind of way. Even Lisa's Dad and I have teased her throughout the years, and I know she understood that it was family teasing and that it was acceptable. But, Lisa also learned when to say, "Stop!" She learned this early on from us, and then as an adult from the workbook and its topic matter on teasing.

At the beginning of the first year in the transitional program, one of Lisa's lessons was to list some of her dreams. She wrote quite a list, which included some of the following: "I want to attend college, get a job in security, child care or in cooking. I want to get an apartment, a two-bedroom with one roommate. I want to wear a uniform, develop friendships and have a boyfriend. I want to have a support system and continue to have contact with my family."

Lisa also had to write what she wanted to be doing in one year and her list was rather short. She said she wanted to still be a part of the transitional program, work somewhere and live at home. Her comments on what she wanted to be doing in five years included living in her own apartment, work somewhere, have friends and visit family. The ten-year plan included a few new activities. Beside the same activities, the hopes and dreams listed above, Lisa added that she would like to "shoot pool, travel and be married." What lofty and worthwhile goals. To her credit, she has achieved most of them.

Over the course of two years, Lisa had a booklet where she and her teachers had listed her best attributes and strengths. They wrote that she was adaptable, accepting, funny, organized, enjoyed singing, dancing and listening to all kinds of music. According to the list, Lisa also liked to lift weights, she got along with others, was friendly, happy, kind and helpful. The teachers also wrote, "she is a 'cool' person, has a good sense of humor, is determined, has a good work history, has had different work experiences and is usually on time. She knows how to tell time, is a fast learner, thinks about answers, processes information, adapts to new things if given time, is aware of things and has the ability to stay on task."

Lisa wrote about what her perfect day might look like, which included this time table: 6 a.m.-get up, get ready on own with alarm clock, 7 a.m.-get ready to go to work (same job all day) Morning-work in security, cooking or child care, noon-lunch with coworkers; Afternoon-work, Evening-come home, cook supper, take a shower, maybe go out-bowling, shopping, to a movie with friends; Bedtime-get ready and go to bed.

And finally, there was a section on Lisa's nightmares. This involved quite a few concerns, some of which I did not know that Lisa had worried about until I read them. The list included: "Leaving home, being alone, being teased, loss of support, the 'system' failing her, being taken advantage of, living at home forever, no-follow though, sitting at home alone, no job coach support, not having services, no future to look forward to, showing up to graduation in my pajamas, having no hopes or dreams, not liking my job, being late to work, the alarm clock failing, not having a ride to work, not having work to do, not having friends, not having money to buy lunch, having a test in the afternoon, having nothing to do in the evenings, having nightmares."

Lisa learned a lot in her two years with this transitional program, increasing and refining skills she already had. She was able to try different jobs to see what would be the best fit for her. She was able to make new friends, learn about interacting with friends and to be a friend. She was getting herself set up for independent living with the help of a variety of household chores that were introduced to her during this two-year program. But, she also learned to have the voice of a self-advocate. She spoke up for her rights and responsibilities, and she was never shy in topics that she held dear to her heart. She learned about herself, and topics such as safe touching. She was able to use this lesson later on, in a situation with a male friend who had made unwelcome advancements and Lisa felt that his actions were very inappropriate. Self-advocacy wasn't taught at this program as a specific course, but rather throughout the time there, Lisa and the other students were made aware of situations that helped them to learn to be good self-advocates.

Because of this, Lisa went on to hold many board positions at the local and state levels, which ran the gamut from secretary to treasurer, then to being Vice-President and President. In particular, the organizations she served on were initially formed because years ago it was deemed necessary to have such positive programs in place that were supportive of the self-advocates and their rights. These important organizations educate people about their rights, helping people with disabilities to be as independent as possible, encouraging others to be able to work in the community at a competitive wage, giving support to those living in the community and making sure their voices are heard.

Meeting new people and making new friends was also a plus. At this transitional program, Lisa knew most of her classmates because they had graduated and moved up to this program at the same time as she did. But, a few students came from other settings, so she was able to meet more people and make new friends. In fact, one of the comments on Lisa's progress report said that Lisa was able to socialize with others, make friends and was very helpful with other students and staff. I realized with comments like that, Lisa was doing well, adjusting, making friends and would be able to move into her own home someday.

There was a lot of variety in this transitional program and Lisa was able to take part, learning as much as was possible in this two-year educational setting. Some of those activities or skill-based learning sessions included cooking classes, learning time as an entire concept, working on math and money skills, exploring community supports, budgeting, learning self-advocacy skills and developing a positive and rewarding friendship circle. The transitional program had a graduation at the end of the two year period, so one of Lisa's grandmothers, as well as Lisa's Dad and I, attended an outdoor celebration. The graduating students, who helped to serve and pick up afterwards, also made the decorations and food. It all looked good and the food tasted great.

Lisa had been doing some vocational training at a cafeteria on a college campus in our town. When her two-year, after high school training was over, the new vocational rehab personnel got things in place to see if Lisa would be hired on at that cafeteria. She was! Her position was "dish-room assistant" and she would start work, Monday through Friday, in the fall. A bonus was that one of her best friends would be working there, too, although Lisa had different hours part of the time. That was a successful placement, because it allowed Lisa to earn a living, use her skills and be a contributing part of the community. Lisa ended up working there for many years. Here is a note she wrote about this job: "I love this place. They told me that I was doing a good job. I'll be working here for about 10 extra years. I really do like the staff." All I can say is "Many thanks" to the efforts of the high school and the transitional program teachers and staff, which allowed Lisa to be so successful.

Youth Leadership Forum

The first Kansas Youth Leadership Forum (KSYLF) was held in 2001. And, that was the year Lisa became involved with the program. In 2005, funding was secured to create a statewide, non-profit organization called the Kansas Youth Empowerment Academy which states: "The KYEA mission is to educate, mentor and support youth with disabilities to be contributing members of their community." [23] This new organization was established to house the KSYLF, as well as other programs that empower young people with disabilities.

When Lisa was involved with the Kansas Youth Leadership Forum, it was a 5 day event in which a selected group of high school students with disabilities stayed on a college campus to learn about leadership, career options, advocacy, goal setting and much more. Those delegates learned through invited speakers, hands-on activities and exposure to successful adults with disabilities. Each year there were approximately 25-30 high school juniors and seniors from across the state that were chosen to participate. It was stated that applicants must possess an interest or potential for leadership and that KSYLF was open to students with any type of disability. Some of the activities included large group sessions with a lecturer, small group sessions, resource fair, Real Life Affair, Day at the Capitol, barbecue, adapted recreation, mentor luncheon, talent show and a dance.

Lisa was involved with the first YLF in 2001, and really enjoyed it once she got settled in. Getting her ready was an unusual atmosphere for me because preparing and packing for the YLF felt like I was sending her off to college. Well, technically she was going to a college, since that is where this group would be staying for five days and four nights. We had to pack all her regular items like clothing, toothbrush and toothpaste, pajamas and other necessities. We also had to furnish a set of twin sheets as well as a towel and hand cloth. We didn't have any twin sheets, so I had to go and buy some. The red sheets and pillowcase were a hit with Lisa. Then Lisa suggested that she needed some snacks, just in case, so I went and bought those. Finally, we had her suitcase packed and the day came for her to leave home and spend the week with others who shared her interest in advocacy and leadership.

She was nervous about attending, about staying in the college dorms and about being away from home. Lisa must have gotten along fairly well and made some kind of an impression because at the end of the week, as I was reading the local newspaper, I came across an article that was written about the recent leadership conference. There was a picture of Lisa, standing on a platform, and it looked like she was talking to a crowd of people. Lisa had been chosen to deliver a thank you for the meal. I didn't hear what she had to say, but I was told she did a great job.

Then, a couple of months after this five day forum, I received an email from the coordinator, who told me more about the experiences she saw with Lisa in attendance. First, this coordinator took the time to say what an inspiration and delight it was to have Lisa at the YLF. She went on to write, "There were times when she (Lisa) struggled with the material and activities, which frustrated her, but she hung in there and gave it her best. You would have been proud. She touched us all and we learned important lessons from her. I was so inspired by the way the other delegates accepted her and supported her and she gave back, in return. I'll never forget how, during the closing ceremony when I was expressing my thanks to the delegates and staff, and she alone walked forward and gave me a hug. It was heartwarming. You are so wise in your parenting. I, too, believe our children live up to our expectations. Far too often kids with disabilities are not challenged to 'stretch' and grow."

The following year, Lisa was asked to speak in front of an organization that the YLF representatives were to attend, to make others aware of the purpose of YLF and to get the word out for the next 5-day forum. A representative from YLF who was in charge sent a letter saying, "Lisa could talk about her experiences of being interviewed and selected, her experiences at the YLF and how that impacted her life." She also wrote "it would also be okay if Lisa wants to talk about some of the challenges she faced...I think it shows the wonderful spirit of determination she has!" Lisa wrote a speech, which I typed up for her to read. She does well speaking her mind, especially when she truly believes in the topic matter, but having the script written must have been helpful. The coordinator wrote this response after the speech was given. "Lisa was awesome! Not only did she do an awesome job, but she also helped to secure $19,500 from the Council for YLF!! I'll have to admit, she made me cry; I was so proud of her. Many thanks to you, your husband and Lisa." This is Lisa's speech.

My name is Lisa Barcus. I was at the Youth Leadership Forum last summer. I was nervous about going and about being away from home for 5 days.

I am glad I went, because I made some new friends and I got to know other people. We played games, learned a lot of things, and shared ideas and dreams.

I learned about computers, assistive technology and many other things in the workshops.

I enjoyed the time that I gave thanks for the food that was provided for us.

When I came home, I felt like the president of the whole world. I wanted my voice to be heard, so I could help kids and adults with special needs. They need help so they can learn on their own and live on their own.

Since being in the Youth Leadership Forum, I was named the self-advocate of the year for the Self-Advocates in my town. And, I was elected to the board position of treasurer for our state, the State's Self-Advocate Coalition.

I hope you will help support the youth leadership forum, so that other kids can attend and become better leaders like me.

Thank you.

The year after that, Lisa had an interest in being a volunteer for the YLF. Again, she had to fill out a form and then she waited to hear if she was accepted. In her form, there was a space to explain why she was interested in volunteering for the YLF. Lisa wrote, "I graduated from the first Youth Leadership Forum and would like to help others have a positive experience." We received a form letter thanking her for her interest, and that there would be an awesome group of volunteers who would attend. Then the following notation made me a little nervous. "Due to the additional security requirements this year, it is taking longer than we anticipated getting all the volunteer background checks completed." Wow, I didn't know about the security checks. But then, I shouldn't have anything to worry about because Lisa had never been in any real trouble with the law or any other things that might make her less awesome. The letter concluded with "If you have received this letter, you have passed the preliminary screening for YLF and have been accepted as a volunteer for the YLF. Congratulations!" Well, why didn't they say that to start with?

Some of the topics and activities they experienced were sessions on Team Building, Discovering My Strengths, Advocating For My Needs, Getting Online, Going to the State Capital and seeing the governor, as well as small breakout groups, a Talent Show and an Ice Cream Social. Lisa came home armed with self-confidence, being a better self-advocate and becoming more open about her opinions. Granted, she was still quiet and reserved, with her soft-spoken voice and sense of shyness about her with strangers, but at home and with family she could take on the world with her great ideas and her strong determination when she wanted to get something done.

In a recap of the five-day experience, the organization mailed a few pages put together in newsletter form that had some comments from those who attended. The sections covered activities that the delegates took part in and they were asked things like, "What activity did you like best?" "What new activity would you like to see for next year?" "What was your favorite part about the forum?" Well, what Lisa voted as her favorite activity was dancing. No surprise there. She has always loved to dance. And a positive comment that was a quote from Lisa: **"I feel more confident when I talk." Lisa, Alumni.** The last bit of correspondence was unexpected but appreciated. The notecard said "Lisa, It was nice meeting you at the YLF mentors luncheon last week. If you have any questions about careers or want to discuss disability issues, please feel free to give me a call." A Legislative Liaison member involved with a state commission on disability concerns program signed it. I was impressed.

Lisa went through a small-group session that had topics that dealt with leadership qualities, as well as issues that pertained to subjects such as personal goals, developments, self-advocacy, finding a purpose and making a difference. Some of the qualities she wrote about herself included the following: "I am patient, I am always organized, I am a risk taker and I am reliable." She also talked about her really super high vision and having a good personality. Other written comments were that she hoped to reach certain goals, help others and she would never give up. She ended one section of this worksheet with, "I am a flexible, creative leader who doesn't give up. As a leader I want to motivate positive thoughts." She not only helped others because of this leadership program, but she boosted her confidence and was able to stand up at meetings and in front of large groups to tell of her story, her hopes and her dreams.

Later on in Lisa's life, when she was asked to give a speech at one of the meetings she regularly attended, she wrote this:

Don't judge people with disabilities, how we interact with each other. Now is not the time to tease people with special needs. Then help them learn about life in the real world. Don't tease kids with learning disabilities. Sometimes we are slow at first. We learn fast if we need help. If we don't know about math or science, we need help. We have to learn to ask for help. Don't hesitate to help, even with special needs or not. If we don't know, spend time and help us learn. I will have time helping people learn how to get ready for the real world. Just help us out to get to know about life or help kids with a hole in their heart to know life, help them out by talking with them when they are listening or not.

Employment Agency

A certified disability-related employment service was utilized when Lisa wanted to have a job after her high school and her community-based trial cafeteria job was over. According to this employment service agency, they had a high success rate in placing people in a suitable and appropriate place of employment and those who benefitted from the training service were very satisfied with the job they were trained to do through this organization. The people served, those with disabilities, were known to have job stability as well as low absenteeism rates. For the businesses, there were also benefits because the new hires would have on-site training with a job coach to help in the initial training process.

Lisa was able to utilize this service, and the result was her first real job, working at the college campus cafeteria. The employment service agency initially began their tests with Lisa by giving Lisa evaluations to see what her interests might be and they did so by using pictures. The pictures showed different jobs, and in the process of this test, the tester could also glean information about how strongly the person liked the different choices presented through the pictures. There were tests that included manual dexterity and coordination issues, a comprehensive assessment in reading and recognition, while another test could score her abilities as well as designating a school grade level. Lisa was also given a self-esteem inventory, which basically asked Lisa questions about how she might handle things, and then those answers were scored.

There was an assessment plan and some vocational objectives decided through a comprehensive, detailed, situational and very diversified array of methods to come to their summary of possible jobs for Lisa. This summary report was over twenty pages long and very detailed in the information. On page three, after the preliminary information was given, there was a list of abilities that Lisa had been tested on and it was noted that she was able to accomplish all twenty items of skills that were tested. Some of the skills listed were as follows: to recognize and discriminate among lowercase and uppercase letters, recognize lowercase sight words, interpret clock time, use simple height and weight tables, count coins and identify the coin type and interpret operating instructions and directions or labels for consumer products if in picture form.

Just below this extensive list, there was a note that was in bold print and underlined, which said: "It is significant to note that Lisa was able to accomplish the entire test without requiring assistance as to reading prompts." That made me proud. Knowing that Lisa could do their testing and not require assistance with the reading. She might have only been reading at a third grade level or so, but she could read, and I felt that all the schooling, all the work she put in and all the support from her teachers was now paying off. A lot of the above listed abilities are the positive result of the two-year community living program from where Lisa had just graduated.

The rest of this long report had situational assessments, gave a recap of where she racked up over twenty-two hours of observation at a variety of trial jobs. Five job placements were assessed, giving a description of the business, a performance summary with a detailed description of the tasks of either one or two days of work at each site. Summaries were listed with comments about how Lisa did, what she needed help with and if this job might be a good fit for her in the work force. The final few pages listed all her employment skills, which ranged from adapting to change, attitude about working, independent work rate, work and schedule preferences and situational barriers such as independent street crossing and travel skills. That list was over thirty-five skills long. There was also a section with each skill that allowed for consumer input, meaning Lisa could comment on what she thought she could do in each employment skill that was presented to her. For her communication skills she reported, "Sometimes it is hard to talk to people I don't know." For time awareness, she would look at her watch and told the time using the sweep second hand, and for the skill of handling feedback and independent street crossing, there was "no comment." The third column had family and staff input. These were very positive, truthful statements about Lisa's abilities.

The final report listed Lisa's interest in the different jobs she might like to have, along with listing her other interests, her outside activities and her prior work history. Her strengths were noted, including positive comments about her ability to "catch on" quickly when tasks were demonstrated, she demonstrated adequate memory recall skills and had endurance and physical stamina for a variety of work environments. She scored above average in self-esteem and demonstrated a very healthy concept as to the opinion of herself. That is one thing I have always seen in Lisa. She has always had an amazing attribute of self-confidence and self-worth. Don't know if we did anything to foster this characteristic, but I am so glad that she has always had such a positive attitude about herself. With all this information, the team that would help Lisa secure a job in the community began to review her options. As it turned out, they didn't have too far to go to achieve that goal. The cafeteria that she had worked at during her last year of the transitional program she attended was willing to hire her on as a paid staff member. It took a little time to get this set up, mostly with the paperwork that goes along with getting a job in the workplace. Lisa worked at this job setting for many years, and was considered an asset to the employer. She had worked in that setting for four years when she received an award for Employee of the Month. One of her supervisor's stated, "Lisa is a valuable employee. She sees we are busy and jumps right in to help." Lisa's comment when interviewed before this award was handed out was, "I love working there." It was a good fit for her for almost eight years.

Health Issues Become Work Issues

Lisa was living in her own apartment, and even though I saw her quite regularly, I never felt that I always had a true picture of how she was doing. This came to light one day when she told me that her stomach had been hurting for a while. I took her to the family doctor who in turn recommended her to a surgeon when lab results showed a high white blood cell count that confirmed an infection. Because Lisa had been sick at work after eating or drinking something, she had to call in sick a couple of times, which was very unlike her to be sick or to miss work. Lisa also had bouts of pain in the upper right abdomen area and back pain, so a visit to the surgeon was the next step to confirm what was the true cause of her symptoms. I am sure they must have done lab work as well, and possibly some comprehensive diagnostic imaging tests such as ultrasound, x-rays or a CT (computed tomography) scan. The CT scan isn't the most effective way to discover gallstones but it can also spot gallbladder problems. And, guess what; it was gallstones.

The decision was made to do surgery, so Lisa was told about the procedure, how long she might be off work and some of the health issues with having her gallbladder out. The medical term is laparoscopic cholecystectomy, which is basically a minimally invasive procedure to remove the gallbladder. In Lisa's case, they removed the gallbladder and gallstones by making a few small incisions in the abdomen. I think she probably stayed in the hospital at least one day and was back at work within a week or so. Well, let's just say she tried to go back to work. We had scheduled the surgery around a time when Lisa's Dad and I were going to be home. But, once she was back at her apartment and things were going good, we went to Hawaii for much anticipated trip that had been planned way before Lisa's gallbladder issues. Her job coach reassured us that Lisa would be back at her cafeteria job, on her regular schedule and for us to not worry. Ya, right.

    I am a worrier and as much as I try not to, I do worry; a lot. And come to find out, my worrying didn't stop what I had feared could happen. Guess worrying really doesn't help. So, it really didn't surprise me when the job coach called me one morning at 4:30 a.m., just a day after we arrived in Hawaii. I was startled at the phone ringing at that time of night, or should I say it was early morning? Then I remembered where the job coach was calling from, the mainland and I knew that it must have been at least 8:30 a.m. there. So, I listened to what was going on with Lisa and then tried to sound like I was awake enough to talk sensibly. Lisa had gone to her job, only to eat something for her breakfast and got sick to her stomach. The job coach made sure she got home okay and then decided to call me. Good call, but I wasn't sure what to say. I think we agreed that medically she would be fine, and that maybe she just needed a different food choice for a few days to help her body adjust to the surgery, partly because of the fact that there was no longer a gallbladder to digest the fatty foods. This strategy was tried, but with little success. Lisa would arrive at work each day, eat, get sick and then get sent home. At some point, it was decided she should go back into the hospital, and I am not sure if it was because her symptoms got worse or what happened. The worst thing was that Lisa's Dad and I weren't home yet from Hawaii. So, we called in reinforcements. Lisa's brother and his wife drove some forty-five minutes to be with Lisa, listened to what the doctors had to say and then gave us a call to tell us of the updates. It was a difficult time for Lisa, her brother and sister-in-law and for Lisa's Dad and I. I think she was only in the hospital a day or two and by then we were back home. Lisa tried to go back to work, but it just wasn't meant to be. So, her job coach recommended that Lisa ask to be released from her job, and on good terms, just in case she would ever want to go back to that establishment to work. It took Lisa awhile to get her body settled and it took longer for her to get a different job, again using the certified disability-related employment service program. In the meantime, she was a part of a community day services program that was offered through another organization.

Over the years, I have had the opportunity to be in different towns and states and was able to see how other community organizations handled the situations or needs that occur when it comes to a person who has a developmental/intellectual disability and who needs a place to be during the day. When Lisa was a baby, she had no need for a service like this, but as she grew older and wanted a job, the conversation would somehow turn to the day services that were available for Lisa. I had always wanted Lisa to have a job, work in the community in some type of work that she liked and that could be rewarding for her. Lisa wanted to work and I felt that was a great attribute and helpful in securing employment. Some organizations that worked in the community helping people with disabilities to obtain a meaningful job would invariably mention day services setting as an option. Early on, I did not like this suggestion because I thought of a sheltered workshop setting, which in my mind wasn't a positive choice. I believe this term had been used to describe the age-old facilities that exclusively or primarily employed people with disabilities. And according to Wikipedia.org (2016) the term 'sheltered workshop' had been used in the past. At some point, there was a replacement term for 'sheltered workshop', which was changed to 'work center'. Either way, I did not have good thoughts about Lisa being in a setting like this. Boy, was I wrong but I finally got my thinking cap on straight. Lisa needed a place to be during the day, at least until she found another job to replace the cafeteria one. So, we went to visit and moved through the process to see if she could be a part of and benefit from that day services center in our local town. This specific organization we looked at was established in 1972, was and still is a not-for-profit organization and has grown over the years, earning a reputation for quality services and care as a community service provider. The mission of this community service provider is to help people with disabilities shape his or her own future. There are a variety of services for those adults who utilize this organization, including case management, health support, work services and residential options. I am so glad we had this option for Lisa and in time it all worked out for her. With the help of a job coach and this community service provider, she did start a new job at a fast food restaurant, is still working there to this day and loves it.

After the paperwork and all that was involved to get Lisa ready, she finally started going to this day service program regularly, enjoying the work and the people who also worked there. This included the super staff members who were working with Lisa and other people who were there because they had a need to be in such a great program. I was glad that we found this program and that Lisa was doing so well. I had to change my way of thinking about this organization. At first, I just thought of it as a place for Lisa to go until she got a new job somewhere, but it is much more than that. It is a place where Lisa *can* go and where she *wants* to go. She has a great group of friends, she is doing important work, earning money while she is working and she has a great routine and camaraderie with those around her in that setting.

The support staff and the services they provide are superb. People are always considerate of our involvement and mindful of Lisa's needs. The staff that helped Lisa have been very kind, thoughtful, understanding and caring. There are a variety of services available, and there are always a variety of events going on within the organization. Such organizations have to rely on state funding and other such ways to amass the money needed to serve those in the community that needs their services.

And, I am sure there are times they don't receive what the organization really needs to provide the services. Lisa's Dad wrote the following letter, to senators and people in congress at a time when there were money issues in the state, and threats of service programs being cut to a bare minimum of support.

"Imagine. You are a young couple in the delivery room. You are feeling the excitement and anticipation at the birth of your child. The baby is born and there is a flurry of activity. Other doctors show up and suddenly the silence seems to go on forever. Then the doctor says, 'You have a daughter. But, there's a problem.' Your life has just taken a new and unexpected path. You're not sure that you can handle being the parent of a child with a disability. Will your daughter be able to live with this disability? You pray, you worry; you search out all the information you can find on this disability. The heart surgery, if needed and if successful, will save her life but what quality of life will she have? You make a lot of decisions that most parents never have to think about. What kind of a life *will* your daughter have?

As the years go by, you watch as a very brave and courageous little person has to struggle through life. You defend her, you encourage her and you do everything within your means to ensure her a life of dignity and independence. Your efforts have not been in vain. Soon, a young adult emerges who is ready to take her place in the world. 'But, there's a problem.'

For all of your efforts and the efforts of the school systems and many other agencies, she is not quite able to do it entirely on her own. Her disability makes it almost impossible for her to handle her own finances. Transportation is another problem. She can't drive and she needs help learning the bus routes and schedules. She has learned to cook a little and take care of her apartment but she still needs reminders and help making some decisions.

Thank heavens for programs that help with these types of situations. You are able to put together a support system that allows your daughter to live independently. You count on these supports being there if something happens to you and your spouse. But, wait. Now you can stop imagining because reality is at the doorstep. Cuts in funding programs are going to have a profound and life altering effect on hundreds of citizens. Instead of requiring a minimum of support to live independently, they will become more of a burden on the state.

We have raised four children with abilities that run from masters' degrees to special education needs. Through all of the ups and downs of career changes and relocations, we were able to satisfy their needs. I wouldn't even attempt to say that their wants were satisfied. I believe the state is faced with this same dilemma. People with disabilities need support. Parents want all their children to have the best education money can buy. You, the people voted in to do the best for our state and its citizens, are faced with some serious problems and any solutions are bound to be unpopular. Please do the right thing to ensure that people's <u>needs</u> are met before the <u>wants</u> eat up the entire budget."

The not-for-profit organization that Lisa was able to be a part of has been a blessing to her and us. They have been there for her when she needed a place to go, when she needed a job and when she needed support while living independently in the community. They gave her the supports needed so she *could* live as independently as possibly. This organization encouraged her independence and self-reliance. They have given Lisa a chance to make her own decisions, make her own way and live a life similar to what we all might like to experience. She has been able to have a job, living in the community and have a successful and rewarding life. It has been a positive and most welcome experience.

Santa Notes From Lisa

Dear Santa, Are you tired of cookies and milk. Instead I will give you a donut and a diet Pepsi.

Dear Santa, I wish that I was stronger. I am fat. Can you help me? I do not like what I'm seeing. I just want to be myself. Please bring some muscles to me. Help yourself to food, except those hot dogs and the beer.

Dear Santa, Please bring me a Christmas gift. I want a kitty.
Dear Santa, Can I have your phone number? Mine is 000-000-0000. Call me some time. This info is for you.

Dear Santa, My grandma gets the coffee. We made chili. P. S. All the kids gave you cookies. Have a safe Christmas. Do you want cheese in your soup?

Dear Santa, I really do believe in you. Enjoy the flight to the North Pole. Can I get a kiss before you go? Ho Ho Ho. Season's greetings.

BARCUS

Dear Santa, I know you are tired of cookies and milk. I believe in you and all your hard work. I'm being really good this year, even with my neighbors. Happy Holidays.

Dear Santa, What do I want for Christmas, you asked. Money. It doesn't matter how much. And new Croc shoes, please. Thank you.

Christmas list: little bigger luggage, hot cocoa set, Bronco's sporting wear, two piece shower set, a bucket of fish

Rap that Lisa wrote in 1998 (going to a new school as a senior)

    Rap of 1998

        Head up, head up is the real world.

        Don't, don't be crazy; taking drugs is stupid.

        Keep, keep kids and learn from me.

        Bad, bad to the bone, be cool, go to school.

        Root, root for me, I'm the best.

        Vote, vote for me as a senior.

        Vice president, I am personable.

        Lisa Barcus, Smartness

A note Lisa wrote before graduation: I dream to graduate, own a cat, have my own place and get a job.

Journal notes written by Lisa: Boys are sweet sometimes. They are flattering; some are hot, some are different. Life is sweet in some ways and also hard. People with disabilities are different in some ways. Never give up hope and thoughts and dreams on kids like us. We are not dumb. We can learn with or without help.

This note Lisa wrote to her Dad when we were planning a picnic. "Dad, is it ok to have a menu made up? Menu: Frozen margaritas, chicken grillers, barbecue chips, coleslaw, pistachio salad, chocolate cake." (I thought that was a great menu, especially the first item!)

BARCUS

I had asked Lisa to check the size of her worn out tennis shoes that she was wearing, so I could look at getting another pair of shoes for her. Lisa's written reply: 6 1/2. Both shoes.

In her daily logbook that was provided by a school she was attending, I had made an entry to the teacher about Lisa losing her activity card that allows the students into the various sports activities. I wanted to know how to obtain a replacement for her. Below my note Lisa wrote, "They are ordered after Christmas in January. They usually cost about $25.00." Under that note, I wrote $25.00 or $5.00. I thought that Lisa had misunderstood the amount the teacher might have mentioned and I also thought that $25.00 was a lot of money for an activity card. Well, Lisa was correct in the amount, but we lucked out, because someone found Lisa's original activity card and it got returned to Lisa. Yay!

Per Lisa's note on "The Life of Me"

I want to see 2001. Can't wait.

I want to be responsible for my actions.

I want to have friends to have fun.

I need to be a grown up.

I want to take care of myself.

I want to be a good friend to others.

I need to enjoy my life.

I want to be a fun person to be with.

I want to be my own self in life first.

I want to live independently on my own.

I want to stand up for myself.

I want to respect others.

I want to speak out for myself and others.

I need to pay bills and taxes.

I want to be strong and healthy for me.

I can be as smart as others are.

I want to be loved by someone.

I want to organize my stuff.

Things to learn:

How to take care of an apartment.

How to push into life.

How to learn to speak out for myself.

How to get along with friends.

How to push away fears.

How to learn what is wrong and right.

How to get my own life.

BARCUS

A few Halloween costumes over the years: A Slice of Bacon, A Princess, Mimi from The Drew Carey Show and Cinderella.

More Notes From Lisa

I want to finish this book on an upbeat note with something funny, humorous and with a light-hearted quality. The following are notes from Lisa, from when she was in middle school, the time she spent in high school and the transitional program. I hope you enjoy them as much as I have over the years. Lisa loves to write poetry and notes. This is her contribution to this book in her own way. Our family has benefited from some of the cutest, ingenious and funny notes from Lisa. Here are a few.

1. Lisa wrote: Leave me a note. I wrote back on the same note: "Here is a note" and I also added a musical note symbol. Lisa wrote back: HA!

2. Happy Birthday, Mom! Run for the hills.

3. Mom, Brent got drunk. He called at 11:18. He'll be home in one hour.

4. Mom, Brent called. Mom, how much is a motorcycle.

5. Adam, I love you as a brother. I want, for your sake, for you to quit smoking. I don't want you to die. Stay alive. I love you big brother.

6. To Mom and Dad: There is no need to wake me. I know you are home. Good night. I love you both.

7. Mom, do you have a key? I will be back later. I'm at I-Hop.

8. Mom, if you feel like yelling, you have my permission.

9. Dad and Brent, Pick up your dishes.

10. Mom, I am sorry. I shouldn't take off. I will tell you who I am with and what time I will be home or I will call. I got the hint. I will be home on time. I love you always. I will make myself go to my room. I should have known better. I will learn. It's hard. Send me to bed without my dinner.

11. From Lisa: There's a picture of a bunny drawn in blue ink, and underneath it, it says "Dad." Then beside it is an equals sign, and then she drew a heart shaped happy face. Lisa writes: You are my hero, Dad. I look up to you as a cool Dad and a Grandpa. You are one handsome Dad. I love you so much.

12. (This was an anniversary card, made by Lisa.) On the front: "Happy, Happy 45th Anniversary." Then, Lisa drew lines under the 45th numbers, and below the word anniversary, and she drew a very nice heart shaped happy face. Inside, she wrote:

Parents, parents, they are my best friends.

Parents, parents know what is best in my life and health.

I love my warm, loving parents.

That's how I know them. Just relax on your day! Congrats.

13. From Lisa and her sister, who probably didn't know about this homemade card: Mother, without a doubt, this is your special moment. Us daughters are your number one on Mother's Day. I'm so proud you are my mama. Hugs and kisses from both of us. Have a

fun time. From your daughters. Thank you for being our mom.

14. Mom, mom, I love my mom. Why do I love mom. She knows what is the best for me, even though I'm the baby, still I love her home cooking. She's my best friend and a power mom. Happy Birthday.

15. Dear Journal, My head is aching with pain with the phone calls from my ex-boyfriend. He gave me a headache. I just wanted to strangle him. We are friends, nothing more and if he thinks it is more, I know karate.

16. A note by Lisa of things she wanted for her birthday- I want these things: sandals, bagel toaster, 12-pack of juice, birthstone ring

17. Dad, can I borrow your truck sweater for tomorrow? I will return it all in one piece. I'll take responsibility for it? (Dad wrote: OK)

18. Lisa called me on April Fool's Day and asked if my refrigerator was running, and then before I could even answer, she responded with, "Well, you better go catch it!"

19. Note from Lisa: Dear Mom and Dad, Happy 30th anniversary. You guys look cute together. You guys are like love birds. Thank you for all the love you give me. I love you guys, the happy couple. Thank you for my special name. You named me Lisa Marie Barcus. Thanks for the love and hope and care of your baby, Lisa Barcus.

20. I am a daughter of two parents. I will check up on my mom when she gets old, 83 or higher. I will help her any way I can. I will hold her hands and feet when she has a fever. I will be there when she walks. I will be in her footsteps and will always be a lot like her. I will help my mom when she gets sick. I will make her a nice cup of hot tea and soup, and wrap her in a blanket.

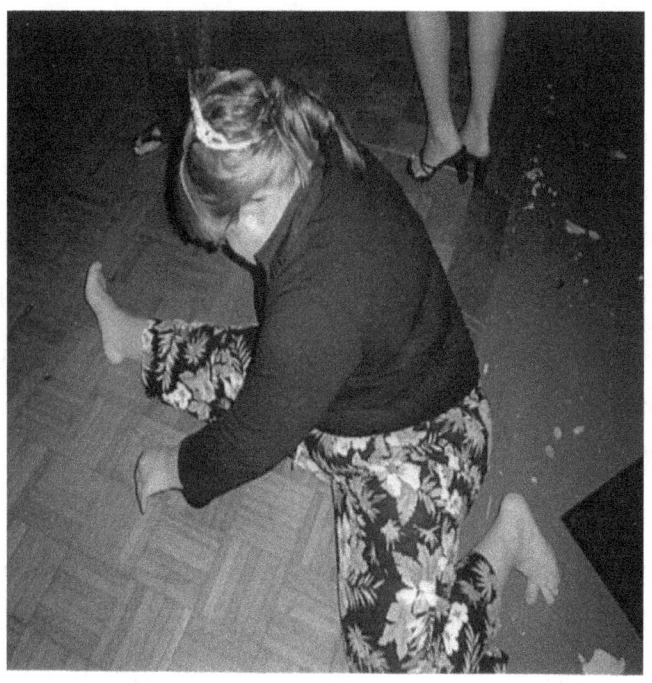

Epilogue

After I published the first book I wrote about Lisa, *Snapshots of Lisa: A Candid Look at Down Syndrome and Snippets of Lisa's Life*, I began reading it to her, so she could hear about all the great and challenging stories in her life. I also started telling her about some of the stories that I would eventually write for the current book you have just finished reading. As with the first book, I wanted to give Lisa the opportunity to approve the articles before I published this second book. I did not want to publish something that she might not want made known to the readers.

I then asked her for comments on the stories and I told her she could share anything she might want to say about the books. Lisa's comments: "I loved the books. Some of these things I'd never known before. I learned a lot about me and a lot of other things, including learning about my parents. They are the best thing about my life. I like that I can share my funny stories and poetry." Then she took the time to write the following: 'I love you, You love me. We are Family. With a hug from me to you, would you say that you love me, too.' By Lisa Barcus

I knew I wanted to end this book with the photo of Lisa doing the splits, first of all because she loves to dance and the splits is always a part of her routine. But, more importantly, I realized that this picture has more meaning than just Lisa doing the splits.

The splits are something that not everyone can or should attempt. I am always impressed when someone does the splits. I did them in my younger years, adding the illusion of flexibility in between my cartwheels and backbends while tumbling in our grassy front yard. It seems that doing the splits may be easy or natural for some people, but not for me. I felt like I spent a lot of time trying to master the art of doing the splits, only to quit practicing after missing out on a position with the high school cheerleading squad. To master the splits, you must always stretch, stay patient and positive. Warm ups, stretches and practicing daily helps. Having a friend to work with you can also be a plus.

Which brings me to my point about liking this photo. Lisa has not only mastered the splits in the physical sense but also in her persistence and determination as she has moved through her middle and high school years of her personal life and life experiences. She has impressed many people along the way with her flexibility and agility when it comes to the many changes she has had to face. It was easy for Lisa to do the splits, with no prior training, encouragement or other outside help. So it is with her personal life. Her Dad and I did not have any prior training in how to raise a child with Down syndrome. We just did what needed to be done, went with our past history with raising children and learned to stretch our ways and views when faced with a difficult situation. Lisa learned and stretched, too.

We all kept a positive attitude, working towards the end result, no matter what the situation. We were able to have a warm up period, when Lisa was first born, then learned about stretching our views and ideas to help the situation at hand and finally, we had to do this over and over and over again. We had many people help us along the way; teachers, doctors, others in our community who had a child with Down syndrome and most importantly, the help we had from all our family.

I looked up the meaning of the splits and I found the following: To split means to divide or separate, to break or burst or disunite. It means to leave out or cut out. This was not the case with our family or the help with had. We were united together, working for a great cause, by helping Lisa to be ready to live on her own. We have accomplished that and much more. Look out world, here she comes.

If you have enjoyed this book, I would appreciate any feedback you may have. You may reach me at abBooks3@gmail.com. All comments or suggestions are welcome. Thanks for reading and please take a few minutes to leave a review on line at https://www.amazon.com. Your honest, positive reviews will help me to reach many more readers.

BARCUS

Reference List

P. 1 [1] In humans, a single transverse palmar crease is a single crease that extends across the palm of the hand, formed by the fusion of the two palmar creases (known in the pseudoscience of palmistry as the "heart line" and the "head line") is found in half of people with Down syndrome. It is also found in 10% of the general population. Because it resembles the usual condition of non-human simians, it is also known as a simian crease or simian line, although these terms have widely fallen out of favor due to their pejorative connotation. Wikipedia 2015

P. 9 [2] Per the Nebraska Health and Human Services System Chronological History: 1985: A law changed the name of Services for Crippled Children to Medically Handicapped Children's Services. http://www.dhhs.ne.gov

P. 11 [3] A History of Name Changes
- 1953 - 1973: National Association for Retarded Children (NARC)
- 1973 - 1981: National Association for Retarded Citizens (NARC)
- 1981 - 1992: Association for Retarded Citizens of the United States (ARC)
- 1992 - Present: The Arc of the United States (The Arc)
  http://www.thearc.org/who-we-are/history/name-change

P. 19 [4] Ventricular Septal Defect (VSD)   http://www.heart.org

P. 24 [5] https://en.wikipedia.org/wiki/Brushfield_spots

P. 27 [6] An Individualized Education Program (IEP) is a written statement of the educational program designed to meet a child's individual needs. Every child who receives special education services must have and IEP. From www.parentcenterhub.org

P. 47 [7] National Down Syndrome Society
http://www.ndss.org/Resources/Wellness/Managing-Behavior

P 48 [8] Homebound instruction can also be referred to as home teaching, home visits and home or hospital instruction. Homebound instruction involves the delivery of educational services by school district personnel within a student's home. This differs from home schooling, which is usually delivered exclusively by a parent. (Zirkel, 2003). www.brainline.org

P. 49 [9] Behavior
http://www.ndss.org/Resources/Wellness/Managing-Behavior/

P. 67 [10] People with disabilities http://www.thearc.org

P. 67 [11] People first language https://en.wikipedia.org/wiki/People-first_language

P. 71 [12] People-First Language: A Partial Glossary of Disability Terms. Institute on Disability/UCED. According to their website, The Institute on Disability was established in 1987 to provide a university-based focus for the improvement of knowledge, policies, and practices related to the lives of people with disabilities and their families and is New Hampshire's University Center for Excellence in Disability. https://iod.unh.edu

P. 73 [13] According to what I remember, DLP, Developmental Learning Program is an educational program for students with disabilities in a regular education setting. Children are with age appropriate peers and they work on an academic and useful daily living skills especially for them on an individual basis. In Lisa's case, her main classroom setting was DLP and at certain times throughout the day she went to a typical, mainstream classroom, depending on the subject.

P. 73 [14] According to what I remember, ILP, Independent Living Program works on the skills someone needs to be able to live independently in life. This may include academic skills that transfer into the real world, such as balancing a check book, making a grocery list, getting a ride using public transportation, how to behave socially and other such important skills that most of us learn as we mature and grow. This includes the academics because if we can't read, write or count money, we probably can't do some of the skills mentioned above.

P. 114 [15] U.S. Department of Education https://www2.ed.gov/

P. 162 [16] The Center for Parent Information and Resources www.parentcenterhub.org

P. 180 [17] Guardianship www.familylawselfhelpcenter.org (under types of guardianship)

P. 180 [18] (under the topic: Does my child need a guardianship? The Voice Newsletter, June 2013-Vol. 7, Issue 5)
http://www.specialneedsalliance.org/

P. 181 [19] (under Purpose and Types of Guardianship, in the section titled: Why Might a guardianship Be Needed?)
http://www.familylawselfhelpcenter.org

P. 185 [20] (under Purpose and Types of Guardianship, in the section titled: Why Might a guardianship Be Needed?)
http://www.familylawselfhelpcenter.org

P. 185 [21] (under the topic: Does my child need a guardianship? The Voice Newsletter, June 2013-Vol. 7, Issue 5)
http://www.specialneedsalliance.org/

P. 200 [22] "Responding to Teasing." This is from 1988 AGS American Guidance Service, Inc. pamphlet

P. 207 [23] Kansas Youth Empowerment Academy www.kyea.org

Resources

The Arc-For People with Intellectual and Developmental Disabilities   http://www.thearc.org

The Arc of Nebraska 3601 Calvert St Ste 25

Lincoln, NE 68506-5797

Website: www.arc-nebraska.org

Facebook: https://www.facebook.com/pages/The-Arc-of-Nebraska/167646211703

Phone: (402) 475-4407

Email: info@arc-nebraska.org Chapter #: 47

The Arc of Douglas County

2518 Ridge Ct Ste 238

Lawrence, KS 66046-4061

Website: www.thearcdcks.org

Facebook: https://www.facebook.com/pages/The-Arc-of-Douglas-County/208030402553129

Business Phone: (785) 749-0121

Chapter Email: bbishop@thearcdcks.org

Chapter #: 594

National Down Syndrome Society, 666 Broadway, 8th Floor, New York, New York, 10012

http://www.ndss.org 1-800-221-4602

National Down Syndrome Congress

30 Mansell Court, Suite 108

Roswell, GA 30076

Toll free, at 1-800-232-NDSC (6372), Monday though Friday from 9:00 AM to 5:30 PM eastern time.

National Association for Down Syndrome

http://www.nads.org

1460 Renaissance Drive

Suite #405

Park Ridge, IL 60068

1-630-325-9112

Down Syndrome Guild of Greater Kansas City

http://www.kcdsg.org

5960 Dearborn St #100, Mission, KS 66202

Phone:(913) 384-4848

BARCUS

Author bio

Angee wrote her first book, *Snapshots Of Lisa: A Candid Look At Down Syndrome and Snippets of Lisa's Life* and has now published a second book about Lisa. In *Loving and Learning: Life with Lisa and Down Syndrome*, Angee shares more of the same about Lisa's younger years and reveals some of the more difficult stories as Lisa finishes high school and moves on to bigger and better life experiences.

Angee Barcus is a wife, mother and writer. She loves to read, and writing helps her to sort out issues that might otherwise fester and linger. Having a child with a disability was the last thing on her mind when Lisa was born. She was thinking more about all the dirty diapers and extra loads of clothes, as well as having to once again function on less hours of sleep at night, when this fourth baby arrived. When Lisa was born, Angee's thoughts were quickly flooded with "what now" notions.

Angee's nursing career allowed her to work in a school system, helping young children with developmental disabilities. This gave her another viewpoint about children with disabilities, which helped her when writing about Lisa.

Angee wrote for a newspaper column for almost two years and enlightened others about disability issues in and around where she lived, alternating those articles with short stories about Lisa. Angee is now working on a third book about Lisa's experiences as she moves into her own apartment, becomes a positive, self advocate role model and has to cope with heath issues that are challenging to manage.